Contents

Acknowledgements

This book would have been a far inferior product if not for the invaluable help of many people at Sonic Foundry. The small thanks we can give here pales in comparison to the contributions each of these individuals has made to this project. First, thanks to the entire engineering staff at Sonic Foundry, not only for being there when we need help and answers, but for the sheer dedication to making the best software anywhere. Thanks to Kevin Canney, Dennis Adams, and Tamara Brognano for their excellent editing work, insightful suggestions, and endless pool of knowledge (which we tapped over and over). Thanks to Dave Hill, Richard Kim, Brian Orr, Tony Jedlovsky, Curt Palmer, Caleb Pourchot, Peter Haller, DeLosse Fussell, Ivan Calderon, and Stephanie Pfeiffer for tirelessly answering our questions, and solidifying our understanding, as well as for challenging us to write a book as good as their software. Thanks to Brad Reinke for making the whole project possible. Thanks to Shane Tracy who helped in more ways than we have room to list here. Thanks to John Allhands for helping us get this book printed and distributed. Thanks to Chris Cain and Trish Morrone for making it all legal. Thanks to Dave Chaimson and Steve Foldvari for handling the marketing chores that we don't understand. Thanks to David Schultz for believing in the project, and pushing for it. Thanks to the excellent Sonic Foundry sales and support staff for keeping us honest.

Gary's dedication

Dedicated to my brother Tom.

Michael's dedication

This book is dedicated to my family for all their love and support, and all the great folks at Sonic Foundry who make this stuff possible.

About the authors

Gary Rebholz and Michael Bryant train Sonic Foundry employees and customers to get the most out of Sonic Foundry products, systems, and services. They are the authors of the popular *SAMS Teach Yourself ACID 3.0 in 24 Hours*. They have written two other books (*SAMS How to Use Macromedia Flash 5*, and *SAMS How to Use HTML and XHTML*), and produced countless tutorials and a wide array of other training materials.

Introduction

The next phase for multimedia

Although the term *multimedia* has been around for several years now, two basic factors drive the fact that the number of people involved in the creation of multimedia is on the rise. First, the demand for a dynamic entertainment and information delivery format is rapidly increasing. People consume audio and video content at the movies, on cable, satellite, and broadcast TV, on their computers at home and work, and even on hand held devices. You find multimedia in your car, 30,000 feet above the earth on a transatlantic flight from New York to Paris, on a kiosk at your local department store, and even in your kitchen. It's everywhere, and it's looks and sounds better than ever. Secondly, the tools needed to create multimedia are now accessible to more content creators than ever before. In the past, it took a great deal of expensive equipment to put together even a simple video or audio production. Then, along came the personal computer, and everything changed. Now, even those with a modest budget can experience broadcast-quality video and CD quality audio.

Putting this power to create compelling, high-quality multimedia in the hands of the professional as well as the hobbyist is what Vegas is all about. If you're a seasoned professional, you'll find Vegas to be an important addition to your arsenal of production tools. In many cases, it may be the only tool you need. If you're new to digital audio and video production, you'll find Vegas amazingly powerful, yet easy to use. You'll find yourself spending more time on the creative aspects of your production, and less time on the mechanics.

Vegas is more than just a nonlinear digital video editor. It's an integrated tool that combines editing, compositing, and titling on the video side, with multitrack recording, mixing, editing, and mastering on the audio side, and allows you to encode it all for multiple delivery formats. Whether you intend to print you production to tape for broadcast delivery, stream it over the Internet, or burn it to CD or DVD, Vegas can help every step of the way.

You also have the freedom to experiment. Since Vegas is a nondestructive editor, you never change your original media no matter how you slice and dice it in your project. Because you can see the results of your edits in real time, you don't have to wonder what it will look like or sound like, or wait to find out. Make a change, try a new filter, add a different transition—you instantly see the results. The road to your creative destination just got shorter.

Vegas provides hardware freedom as well. You don't need to purchase additional or special hardware to get up and running. A typical business PC fresh off the show room floor is more than likely way above the minimum hardware requirements. Just capture your video and start editing. The same goes for audio. As long as your sound card is Windows compatible you're ready to record, edit, master, and burn a Red Book standard audio CD. That's right. Vegas Video has more audio power, tools, and capabilities than most dedicated audio software.

If you want to move beyond simple multimedia into the realm of rich media, Vegas Video stands ready to take you there. Rich media is a combination of audio, video, and supporting collateral information. Vegas Video enables you to embed metadata into the finished product. Metadata can take many forms, from simple location markers, which allow the user to navigate through the media in an interactive fashion, to command markers, which synchronize and issue browser commands with the playback of the streaming media. Metadata really puts the *multi* in multimedia, and brings a full rich, interactive experience to those who consume your productions.

We've written this book for multimedia enthusiasts of all levels. Advanced users will pick up tips and tricks even in the basic sections, while beginners will find even the advanced topics easy to understand. We clearly define new terms when we use them. Every lesson contains plenty of step-by-step tasks that solidify the concepts discussed in that lesson. The included CD-ROM contains all the media and project files you'll need to complete the tasks. We've included a healthy number of "Private Tutors" (like the one below) to further explain concepts, explore related topics, suggest further resources, and share tips and power-user techniques. This is a hands-on book. You'll learn by doing— and that's the best way to learn. Open the book, open Vegas, and start editing video and audio right away. Use the techniques we teach here, even as you learn them.

pt **Private Tutor: Completing the tasks**
Video makes extremely high demands on your computer processor.
Therefore, we suggest that you copy the projects (lesson files) and sample
media files that are used in the tasks to your hard drive for better performance.

The book is divided into eight modules. Module 1 introduces the Vegas Video interface and takes you through the process of customizing the workspace to meet your individual needs. In Module 2, you learn how to preview and add audio and Video media to your project. Module 3 introduces some advanced methods of adding media to your projects. It shows how to use a video capture utility, and how to record audio directly into a project. Module 4 concentrates on generated media such as text, scrolling credits, and background elements, and teaches some very important concepts that you will use often. In Module 5, you learn advanced navigation techniques, as well as how to use loop mode and some useful keyboard shortcuts. Module 6 discuses the basic editing techniques you will use in every project. Module 7 covers some fun stuff such as transitions, slow/fast motion, filters and effects, as well as basic audio mixing techniques. Module 8 wraps the whole thing up with a discussion of how to save and render your project, and add metadata to create a rich media presentation.

These eight modules give you a solid foundation upon which you can build your knowledge and expertise with this powerful multimedia creation tool. Throughout the book we give you very specific step-by-step instructions on how to achieve results. We give you the base knowledge you can use to explore the application further and uncover even more advanced techniques. Pop the hood and take a good look around. The more familiar you become with all of the filters, effects, envelopes, and encoding features, the more creative ideas will present themselves to you. Your only bounds are defined by the limits of your creativity. You may very well find ways to use this software that haven't been thought of yet. If you do, don't forget to tell your fellow Vegas users—and us!

We hope you enjoy reading the book, and working through the sample projects in each module. Now, let's dive in and create some rich multimedia with Vegas!

Gary Rebholz
Michael Bryant

Module 01: The Vegas interface

Before you get started using Vegas, you'll need to spend a few minutes familiarizing yourself with the program's user interface. If you're already familiar with other Sonic Foundry products, such as ACID PRO™ or Sound Forge®, you'll feel right at home with Vegas. Even if you haven't used Sonic Foundry products before, a little general knowledge and experience with the Windows operating system helps you quickly become comfortable using Vegas. This module familiarizes you with the three general sections of the Vegas user interface.

In this module you'll do the following:

- Explore the Vegas menus and buttons.
- Learn about the track list and timeline areas.
- Work with the window docking area.
- Discover techniques for customizing your Vegas workspace.

Lesson 1: Menus

The top section of the Vegas screen contains menus and buttons that work just like those in other Windows programs. In fact, some of the commands and buttons are identical to those that you probably already use in your favorite word processing program (as an example). Other commands and buttons are common to Sonic Foundry products, so you may already be familiar with some of them. Finally, some of the commands and buttons are specific to Vegas, and therefore may not look familiar to you at all. The tasks in this lesson concentrate on the menu bar, and the next lesson focuses on the toolbar.

There are multiple ways to access most features of Vegas. Perhaps the most basic method is through commands. The following list summarizes each menu and the general function of the most important commands found beneath it.

- File menu: Create new projects, open existing projects, close projects, and save projects. Import media into your project and access project properties.
- Edit menu: Select basic editing functions such as cut, copy, and paste. Choose editing tools.
- View menu: Show and hide various objects and windows.
- Insert menu: Insert objects and controls (such as new tracks, media, markers, and more).
- Tools menu: Access editing tools and tools for special functions.
- Options menu: Customize certain behaviors of Vegas. Enable/disable snapping, define grid spacing, ruler format, and more. Access Vegas preferences.
- Help menu: Access resources for ideas, definitions, and assistance. Register and access the Sonic Foundry Web site.

pt **Private Tutor: Keyboard shortcuts and accelerators**

Many of the commands in Vegas have keyboard equivalents, or shortcuts. Keyboard shortcuts can increase your efficiency tremendously, so it's a good idea to learn the shortcuts for the operations you perform most often. For commands that have an associated keyboard shortcut, the shortcut appears to the right of the command in the menu. For example, arguably the most important shortcut to learn is for the Save command under the File menu: **Ctrl+S**. You don't have to stop and memorize them all right now. We'll mention those we feel are most useful as we explain the various functions they perform.

Although we don't mention them specifically, there are also keyboard accelerators associated with many menu commands. Vegas underscores one letter from each menu to indicate which letter acts as the accelerator (in Windows 2000 and XP, hold the **Alt** key to see the underscores). Type the underscored letter to open the associated menu. With the menu open, type the underscored letter for the command you want to choose from the list.

Task 1: Using Vegas menus

This task shows you how to use the File menu to open and close an existing Vegas project.

1. In Vegas, choose **File | Open** to display the Open dialog. Alternatively, press **Ctrl+O** on your computer keyboard.
2. In the Look in drop-down list, navigate to the CD-ROM that accompanies this book. (We suggest you copy the contents of the companion CD-ROM to your local machine for the best results with the lessons in this book.)
3. Navigate to the *LessonFiles\Module01* folder.
4. Select *M01Task001.veg*.
5. Click the **Open** button.
6. After the project opens, choose **File | Close** to close it.

Lesson 2: Toolbar

The Vegas toolbar, shown in **Figure 1.1**, provides alternative methods of completing many of the same tasks found in the menus.

Figure 1.1

The Vegas toolbar provides quick access to frequently used commands.

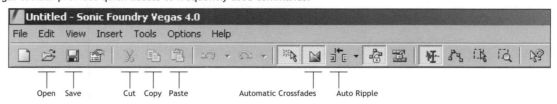

Many of the toolbar buttons should look quite familiar to you. For instance, most Windows programs use the same icons for the **Open**, **Save**, **Cut**, **Copy**, and **Paste** buttons. Other buttons are specific to Vegas such as the **Automatic Crossfades** and **Auto Ripple** buttons. To perform the action associated with a button, click the button.

pt **Private Tutor: Customizing the toolbar**

You can customize the toolbar so that it contains the buttons you use most often. To do so, choose **Options | Customize Toolbar**. In the *Customize Toolbar* dialog, select the button in the left pane that you want to add to the toolbar and click **Add**. To remove a button from the toolbar, select the button in the right pane and click **Remove**. To change the order of the buttons in the toolbar, select the button you want to move, then click **Move Up** to move the button one position earlier in the bar or **Move Down** to move it one position later. Click **Reset** to return the toolbar to its default state. When you're done with your adjustments, click **Close** to dismiss the *Customize Toolbar* dialog.

pt **Private Tutor: Button ToolTips**

Every button has a ToolTip that tells you the name of the button as well as the keyboard shortcut for that button (if one exists). If you are not sure what a button does, hover your mouse over the button until the ToolTip appears. This is also a great way to learn the keyboard shortcuts for the buttons that you use most often.

Task 2: Using Vegas buttons

Now use the Vegas buttons to open another project file.

1. Click the **Open** button in the Vegas toolbar.
2. In the **Open** dialog, navigate to the *LessonFiles\ Module01* folder, and open *M01Task002.veg*.
3. Since there is no button available to close a project, choose **File | Close**.

Lesson 3: Track list area

Below the menu/toolbar area is the main Vegas workspace, shown in **Figure 1.2**. This area contains two sections: the track list area and the timeline (sometimes referred to as the track view area). In this lesson, you'll learn about the track list area.

Figure 1.2

The main Vegas workspace contains the track list area and the timeline.

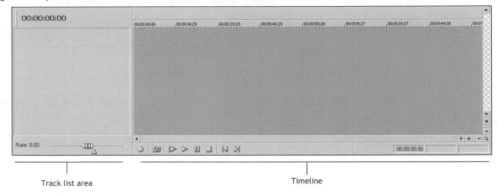

Track list area   Timeline

If you have not added any tracks to your project, the track list (on the left side of the main workspace) is blank. When you add a track to your project, a track header appears in the track list. The track header, shown in **Figure 1.3**, contains controls that enable you to adjust the behavior of the track. For instance, you can mute or solo the track, change the track color, maximize or minimize the track, and perform various other tasks.

Figure 1.3

Track headers contain controls used to adjust track behavior.

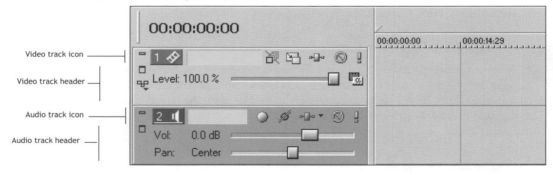

The typical Vegas project contains two types of tracks—video and audio. While the track headers for both of these track types share certain controls, some are specific to the track type. You'll use track headers to adjust many of the parameters of individual tracks in your projects to achieve the audio and video effects you want to create.

> *pt* **Private Tutor: Hiding the track list**
>
> If you want to hide the track list temporarily to gain more workspace in the timeline, press **Shift+F11**. Press **Shift+F11** again to show the track list.

Task 3: Selecting a track for editing

This task shows you how to use the track header to select a track that you want to edit.

1. Use either of the methods you learned in the previous two tasks to navigate to the *LessonFiles\Module01* folder, and open *M01Task003.veg*.
2. This project contains two tracks. As shown in Figure 1.3, the track icons identify track 1 as a video track and track 2 as an audio track.
3. Compare the buttons and controls on the two tracks. While some of them are the same for both track types, differences exist. You'll quickly become familiar with these differences, and soon be able to identify audio or video tracks instantly by the controls present on the track header.
4. Notice that the shading for track 1 differs from the shading for track 2. The darker shading identifies the selected track.
5. Click the track icon for track 2. Now the track shading indicates that you have selected track 2.

pt   **Private Tutor: Scrolling through track headers**

Once you click a track icon to select the track, you can use your **Up** and **Down Arrow** keys to scroll through the track headers in your project. Press the **Up Arrow** key to select the track directly above the currently selected track and the **Down Arrow** to select the track directly below the currently selected track. Remember that you must first select a track. Then you can scroll through the other tracks in your project using the arrow keys as discussed here.

Lesson 4: Timeline

The timeline, shown in **Figure 1.4**, lies to the right of the track list. The timeline holds all of the information regarding what video and/or audio files should play during a specific point in the project. There is, of course, much, much more to the timeline than that, and you'll learn about the powerful editing that you can perform in the timeline in later lessons.

Figure 1.4
The timeline is where most of the action takes place when you're building your projects.

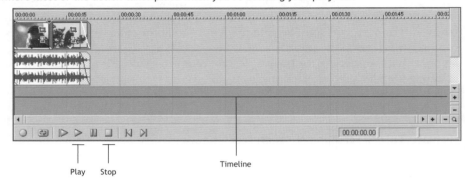

Play   Stop   Timeline

Task 4: Starting and stopping project playback

This task shows you how to use the buttons at the bottom of the timeline to control the playback of your project. Figure 1.4 shows the **Play** and **Stop** buttons in the Transport toolbar.

1. Navigate to the *LessonFiles\Module01* folder on the companion CD and open *M01Task004.veg*
2. Hover over the **Play** button until its ToolTip appears. From the ToolTip, make note of the keyboard equivalent (the Spacebar).
3. Click the **Play** button to begin project playback.
4. The video track shows thumbnails of the video that appears in the Video Preview window, and the audio track contains the waveform for the audio that you hear. As the project plays, the cursor moves along to indicate the exact spot currently playing.
5. Hover over the **Stop** button. Its keyboard equivalent is also the Spacebar. Click the **Stop** button to stop project playback.

pt **Private Tutor: Maximizing the track view**

Very often you'll want to concentrate on the information in the track view. As your project grows, you may frequently wish you had more space for the timeline. To accomplish this quickly, press Ctrl+F11 to hide both the track list and the window docking area. Press Ctrl+F11 to show the hidden areas.

pt **Private Tutor: Resizing the track list and track view**

Hover over the bar that separates the track list from the track view. The pointer changes to the Resize Window icon: ◄╟►. Drag the bar to a new position to change the width of the track list and the track view. Drag the bar that separates the top of the window docking area (discussed in the following lesson) from the track list/timline to change the height of these areas.

Lesson 5: Window docking area

The bottom of the Vegas window contains the window docking area. The window docking area provides a place to store the many windows that you will use while working on your Vegas projects. By default, three windows appear in separate sections of the window docking area: the Explorer window on the left, the Mixer window in the middle, and the Video Preview window on the right. We'll talk in more detail about these in later lessons.

Many windows can be docked in the window docking area. The second section of the View menu lists most of these windows. Choose a window name from the list to close it if it is open (open windows have a check mark before their name), or open it if it is closed.

Task 5: Opening and closing Vegas windows

This task shows you how to use the View menu to open a closed window and two methods you can use to close an open window.

1. In any Vegas project (even a new, blank project), choose **View | Video Preview** to close the Video Preview window.
2. Choose **View | Video Preview** again to reopen the Video Preview window.
3. A **Close** button appears in the upper left-hand corner of each of the windows in the window docking area. Click the **Close** button for the Video Preview window to close it.
4. Press **Alt+6** to reopen the Video Preview window. Note that **Alt+6** also gives focus to the Video Preview window if it does not currently have focus. The keyboard shortcuts for all of the other windows work the same way.

In addition to the three windows mentioned previously, many other windows are open by default as indicated by the check mark next to the window name in the View menu. However, the Explorer window obscures these additional windows. Tabs for each window appear at the bottom of the window docking area as shown in **Figure 1.5**. Click a tab to see its associated window.

Figure 1.5
Click on the tab at the bottom of the window docking area to access the associated window.

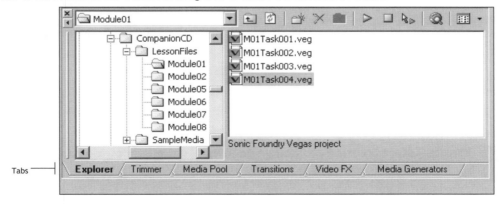

Task 6: Viewing obscured windows

This task shows you how to view windows that are obscured by another window in the window docking area.

1. In any Vegas project (even a new, blank project), notice that there are several tabs below the Explorer window indicating that several windows are hidden.
2. Click the **Transitions** tab to bring the Transitions window forward. The Transitions window now hides the Explorer (and other) windows.
3. Click the Explorer tab to bring the Explorer window to the front again.

The window docking area can contain as many sections as you want. Windows can also be "torn" out of the window docking area to float freely anywhere on your screen (or a second screen if you use dual monitors). To move a window, drag the vertical bar at the left edge of the window. To create a new section in the window docking area, drag the window to a spot between two existing sections. To set the window to float freely, drag it away from the window docking area, as shown in **Figure 1.6**.

Figure 1.6

Drag a window away from the window docking area to allow it to float over another area of the screen.

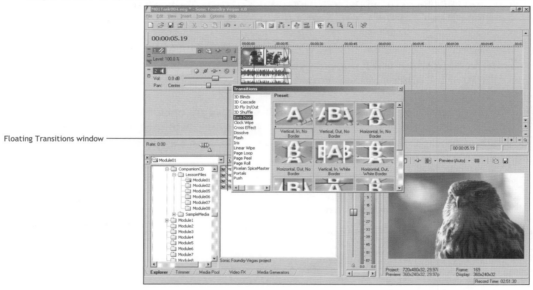

Floating Transitions window

Private Tutor: Creating a floating window over the window docking area

pt

As soon as you drag a window over the window docking area, Vegas prepares to dock the window. To prevent a window from docking when you drop it in the window docking area, press the Ctrl key when you drop the window.

Task 7: Repositioning dockable windows

This task shows you how to create a new section in the window docking area, how to create a floating window, and how to return a window to the window docking area.

1. In any Vegas project (even a new, blank project), drag the vertical bar at the left edge of the Explorer window to the right until it's about halfway between its original position and the Mixer window.
2. Release the mouse button.
3. A new section of the window docking area now holds the Explorer Window.
4. Drag the vertical bar for the Explorer window to the project timeline.
5. Release the mouse button and notice that the Explorer window now floats freely above the Vegas workspace.
6. Drag the Explorer window's title bar to reposition the window, and drop the Explorer window back to its original position in the window docking area.

From time to time, you may want a docked window to be larger so that you can see more of the information it holds. You can adjust the width and height of the window docking area and each section within the area, or you can maximize any window so that it fills the entire window docking area.

Task 8: Resizing dockable windows

This task shows how to resize a window in the window docking area.

1. In the Explorer window of any Vegas project (even a new, blank project), click the **Maximize** button just below the **Close** button. This maximizes the Explorer window. Every window in the window docking area has a Maximize button.
2. Click the button again to restore the Explorer window to its previous size.
3. Hover your mouse over the bar that separates the Explorer window from the Mixer window. The pointer changes to the resize icon.
4. Drag the bar to a new position.
5. Drag the bar that separates the top of the Explorer window and the track list/timeline.

Private Tutor: Hiding the window docking area

To hide the window docking area, press F11. Press F11 again to show the window docking area.

Conclusion

The lessons in this first module have focused on familiarizing you with the Vegas interface. You now know how to use menus and buttons, have a basic understanding of the track list and timeline, and have become familiar with the window docking area. You also learned how to resize areas, hide and show areas, and show, hide, dock, and undock windows to customize your workspace. In the next module, you'll add media files to your project.

Exercises

1. True or false: The Vegas interface follows many of the standards established by the Windows operating system so that many parts of it have a familiar look.

2. Which two of the following techniques can be used to open an existing project in Vegas.

   a. Choose File | Open.

   b. Double-click a blank area of the track list.

   c. Click the Open button.

   d. Choose Help | Find and Open File.

3. True or false: A track header's sole purpose is to identify a track as a video or audio track.

4. Which two of the methods below allow you to select a track?

   a. Drag a marquee around the entire track.

   b. Choose **Select | Track**.

   c. Click the track icon.

   d. Click a track icon, and then press the **Up** or **Down Arrow** key.

5. True or false: The Spacebar starts project playback.

6. True or false: The Spacebar stops project playback.

7. Which of the methods below can be used to close the docked Explorer window?

   a. Choose **File | Close**.

   b. Click the **Close** button at the top-left corner of the window.

   c. Choose **Window | Close | Explorer**.

   d. Choose **View | Explorer**.

8. True or false: Each section of the window docking area can hold exactly one window.

9. True or false: Once a window is docked, it must remain docked until you are done with your Vegas project.

10. Draw a line connecting the keyboard shortcut to the action it performs:

    a. **F11**   Maximize the timeline.

    b. **Ctrl+F11**   Save the project.

    c. **Ctrl+S**   Show the Video Preview window.

    d. **Ctrl+O**   Hide the window docking area.

    e. **Alt+6**   Open a project.

Essays

1. Briefly explain the concept of keyboard shortcuts. Describe not only why you would want to learn them, but also one way to use the Vegas interface as a tool for discovering new keyboard shortcuts.

Module 2: Adding media to your project—basic methods

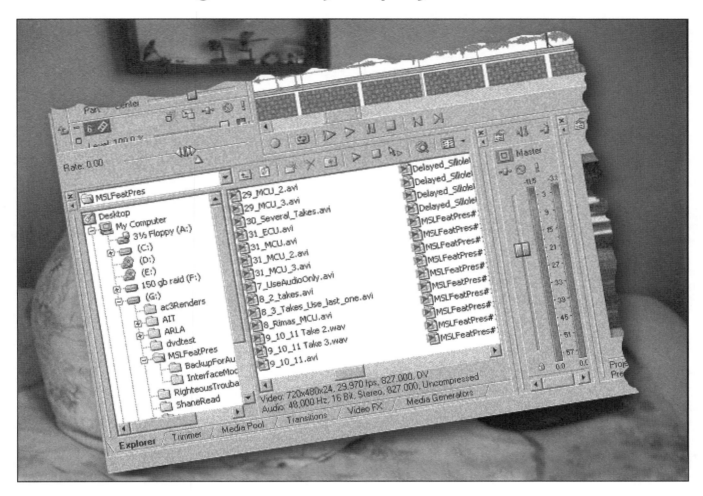

In this module, you'll learn techniques for adding media to your project. The term *media* refers to the pieces and parts you use to construct your project. Media comes in two general forms: audio and video. You'll learn in this module that the techniques for adding both of these types of media are exactly the same, and you will just as easily add a movie clip to your project as a musical soundtrack.

Before you add media to your project, you need to understand more about the Explorer window, so this module starts at that point. From there, you'll explore supported media file types, learn how to preview the media you are considering before adding it to your project, and how to add the media to your timeline.

In this module you'll do the following:

- Learn in detail how to use the Explorer window.
- Discover which file formats you can use in your project.
- Preview your media before adding it to your project.
- Manipulate the project cursor in order to set the insertion point for adding your media.
- Add audio and video media to your project.
- Create new tracks in your project.

Lesson 1: The Explorer window

The Explorer window appears by default in the window docking area at the bottom of the screen. You can use the Explorer window to search for, navigate to, preview, and add media files to your project, all without ever leaving Vegas. You can also create folders and a favorites list, rename, delete, and organize files, and perform other file-management functions through the Explorer window. If you already know how to find files on your computer using the Windows Explorer, then you already know much of what you need to know about the Explorer window in Vegas because the two function almost identically.

By default, the Vegas Explorer window, shown in **Figure 2.1**, displays three sections. The top section contains navigational tools and buttons. Under these tools, a panel on the left shows a tree view of your computer's folder structure, and a panel on the right shows the contents (list view) of the folder selected in the tree view.

Figure 2.1

Use the Explorer window to add media to your project.

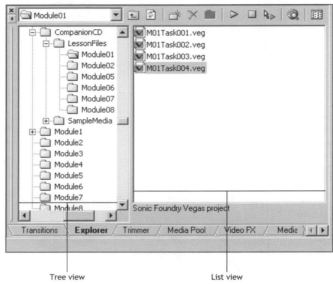

Tree view   List view

Task 1: Navigating to your media

This task shows you how to navigate to a folder that contains media to use in your Vegas projects. You'll notice how similar this process is to navigating to files on your computer system using Windows Explorer.

1. In the tree view section of the Explorer window, click the Desktop icon. In the list view section on the right, you see the details of your Windows desktop, including any shortcuts.
2. If the contents list of the My Computer icon is not expanded, click on the Plus sign (+) in front of the icon.
3. If the contents list of the D: drive (or the drive that holds the CD-ROM that accompanies this book) is not expanded, click the Plus sign in front of the icon.
4. Click the Plus sign in front of the Sample Media folder in the tree view.
5. Click the Video folder. Notice that the contents of the Video folder now appear in the list view section of the Explorer window, showing all of the sample video files on the companion CD-ROM.
6. Click the file Eaglefly2.avi to select it.

The first tool in the Explorer window, the **Address Bar**, gives you a way to find out where you currently are in your computer's file structure. Next, the **Up One Level** button (**Figure 2.2** shows the buttons discussed here) moves up one level in your file hierarchy—in other words, up one level in the path listed in the Address Bar.

Figure 2.2
The Explorer window toolbar.

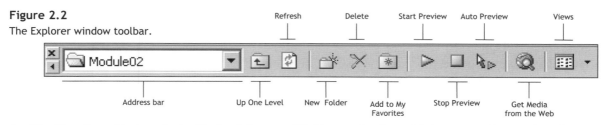

Next to the **Up One Level** button is the **Refresh** button. We'll come back to this important button in a few moments. For now, let's skip to the **New Folder** and **Delete** buttons. These buttons create a new folder or delete a file or folder.

The **Add to My Favorites** button allows you to create a list of shortcuts to folders you use often during the course of your projects. Once you've added a folder to your favorites list, expand the *Desktop* icon in the tree view, and then click the *My Favorites* icon to access the folder you added.

> ***pt*** **Private Tutor: File management in the Explorer window**
>
> Since the Explorer window works so much like Windows Explorer, many of the same options are available in both. For instance, right-click a file in the list view of the Explorer window to view a number of options related to file management. You can rename files, check file properties, delete files, and more—just as you can within Windows Explorer. Right-click a blank area of the list view to access shortcuts to many of the buttons available at the top of the window.

> ***pt*** **Private Tutor: Changing your file structure**
>
> Any changes you make to your computer's file structure from the Vegas Explorer window are made to your computer hard drive or network folder. In other words, making a change (such as adding or deleting a folder) in the Explorer window has exactly the same effect as using Windows Explorer tools to make the change. The exception to this rule is the **Add to My Favorites** button. This list of shortcuts is a list that resides only within Vegas and has no effect on your computer's file structure.

You'll explore the next three buttons during Lesson 2 of this module, *Previewing Media*. For now, let's move to the last two buttons. The **Get Media from the Web** button allows you to start your browser and surf the Internet for resources you can use in your movies. Of course, you must have a connection to the Internet to use this feature.

The **Views** button adjusts the layout of the Explorer window. Click the arrow at the right edge of the button to display the **Views** drop-down. The following options are available:

- **Tree View**: Toggles the tree view section of the Explorer window on and off.
- **Region View**: Toggles the region view on and off. We'll talk about regions in detail later. For now, it is enough to know that some media files contain specified areas (called regions) that can help organize your work. If a file contains regions, the regions appear in the region view section when you choose the file in the Explorer window.
- **Summary View**: Toggles the summary view on and off. With the summary view on, details about a media file appear at the bottom of the Explorer window when you choose the file.
- **Details**: Toggles the details view on and off. The details view gives you extended information about the selected file such as size, type, and so on.
- **All Files**: Toggles between showing only the files Vegas can read (in the off state), and all files in a given folder regardless of whether Vegas can read them or not (in the on state).

Click the main portion of the **View** button to toggle through the four combinations of the first two options in the drop-down.

Now let's return to the **Refresh** button. The **Refresh** button ensures that the Explorer window always shows the current contents of a folder. For instance, if you have a folder open in the Explorer window and add or delete something from that folder using Windows Explorer, the change is not automatically updated in Vegas because Windows Explorer cannot inform Vegas of the change. In cases like this, click the **Refresh** button to instruct Vegas to check the file structure and reflect the appropriate changes.

Task 2: File management with the Explorer window

This task familiarizes you with the Explorer window. In it, you will perform a bit of file management.

1. In the Vegas Explorer window, use the Address Bar drop-down to navigate to your computer desktop.
2. Click the icon for the *My Documents* folder in the tree view. The list view now shows the files and folders that exist within your *My Documents* folder (which may be empty on your computer).
3. Switch to Windows Explorer and create a new folder within *My Documents* called *VegasTestFolder*.
4. Switch back to Vegas. Notice that the Vegas Explorer window does not display the new folder.
5. Click the **Refresh** button. Now the *VegasTestFolder* appears in the list view of the Explorer window.
6. Right-click the *VegasTestFolder* in the Vegas Explorer window, and then choose **Rename** from the shortcut menu. Name the folder *DeleteFromVegas*. Switch back to Windows Explorer and notice that the Windows Explorer reflects the change immediately.
7. Switch back to Vegas and click the *DeleteFromVegas* folder in the list view.
8. Click the **Delete** button. In the dialog that appears, click **Yes** to confirm that you want to delete the folder.
9. Switch back to Windows Explorer, and notice that the folder has been deleted.
10. The Windows Recycle Bin now contains the folder just as if you deleted the folder using Windows Explorer.

Lesson 2: Previewing media

In this lesson, you'll preview files to consider whether or not to add them to your project. In the process, you'll learn about many of the file formats supported by Vegas.

In most cases, you'll use the Vegas Explorer window to add files to your project. The Explorer window provides an easy way to preview your files before you add them to your project.

Let's start with video files. Navigate to the *SampleMedia\Video* folder on the companion CD-ROM. The list view of the Explorer window shows that the Video folder holds several video files.

Vegas can import the following video file formats:

- **.avi**—Microsoft Video for Windows.
- **.mov**—Apple QuickTime movie.
- **.mpg**—Motion Pictures Expert Group. Both MPEG-1 and MPEG-2. You must register your software to gain this functionality.
- **.wmv**—Windows Media Video.

Those of you who have worked with video in the past recognize this as an impressive list of video files. Even more impressive, all can be added painlessly to the same project—in fact, even to the same video track if you want—without any extra work to first transform them into a common format.

Recall that in the previous lesson we neglected to talk about three of the buttons in the Explorer window. Use these buttons to preview your files in the Video Preview window. With a video file selected (and assuming you have not added any media to your project), notice that the Video Preview window is black. Click the **Start Preview** button to preview the selected file in the Video Preview window. Click the **Stop Preview** button to stop the preview. Click the **Auto Preview** button and select another video file in the list view of the Explorer window—the file previews automatically.

task Task 3: Previewing video files

This task shows you how to use the three preview-related buttons in the Explorer window to preview video files in the Video Preview window before you add them to your project.

1. Use the techniques you learned in Lesson 1, *The Explorer window* to navigate to the *SampleMedia\Video* folder
2. Select eaglefly2.avi.
3. Click the **Start Preview** button, and watch the file in the Video Preview window.
4. If *eaglefly2.avi* has already finished playing, click the **Start Preview** button again, and before the video ends, click the **Stop Preview** button to end preview playback.
5. Click the **Auto Preview** button to turn on the automatic preview function.
6. Select *hawkMed.avi* and notice that the file begins to preview automatically. Click another file and it previews automatically too.
7. Click the **Auto Preview** button again to turn off automatic preview mode.

In addition to video files, Vegas supports several still image file formats so you can easily add still images to your project. Vegas can import the following still file formats:

- **.bmp**—Windows Bitmap.
- **.gif**—CompuServe Graphics Interchange Format (stills and animated).
- **.jpg**—Joint Picture Experts Group.
- **.png**—Portable Network Graphics.
- **.psd**—Adobe Photoshop.
- **.tga**—Targa.
- **.tif**—Tagged Image File Format.

Again, this list includes most commonly used file formats, including both of the popular file formats for the World Wide Web (.gif and .jpg). This allows you to download images from the Web (assuming you have permission from the copyright holder) for use in your projects. Vegas also supports the transparency settings of file formats that provide transparency (such as .gif and .png).

To preview a still image file, follow the same procedure as outlined in Task 3.

> ### *pt* Private Tutor: Combining video files with still images
>
> You don't need to do anything special for Vegas to use your still images in the same project as your video files. In fact, you can mix and match any combination of videos and still images in one project, even on the same track. In Vegas, you spend less time worrying about file formats so that you can get on with the job of editing your project. This is a big help when you work with media that comes from a wide variety of sources and in a wide variety of formats.

By now you've probably already guessed that Vegas supports numerous audio file formats too. Vegas can import the following audio file formats:

- **.aif**—Macintosh Audio Interchange Format.
- **.mp3**—MPEG-1 Layer 3.
- **.ogg**—Ogg Vorbis.
- **.pca**—Sonic Foundry Perfect Clarity Audio™.
- **.w64**—Sonic Foundry Wave 64.
- **.wav**—Microsoft Wave.
- **.wma**—Microsoft Windows Media Audio

Now you're getting the hang of previewing files in Vegas. Follow the same procedure to preview your audio files. Obviously, with audio files you hear the preview as opposed to seeing it. You control the preview volume with the Preview fader. To see the Preview fader, choose **View | Mixer Preview Fader**.

Task 4: Previewing audio files

This task shows you how to preview audio files and how to adjust the volume of the preview to a comfortable listening level.

1. Use the techniques you learned in Lesson 1, *The Explorer window* to navigate to the *SampleMedia\Audio* folder.
2. In the list view of the Explorer window, select *DarkContinent.wav*.
3. Use the three preview buttons to control the preview playback of the file.
4. Choose **View | Mixer Preview Fader** and notice that the Preview fader now appears in the Mixer window as shown in **Figure 2.3**.
5. While the file plays, drag the volume slider up to increase the preview volume or down to decrease the volume. Notice that the volume meters give you a visual representation of the volume of the file.
6. When finished previewing the file, choose **View | Mixer Preview Fader** to hide the preview fader again.

Figure 2.3
The Preview fader allows you to monitor and adjust
the volume of the audio you are previewing.

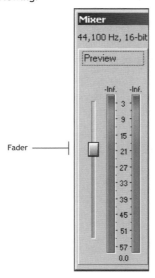

Lesson 3: Repositioning the project cursor

You're getting very close to adding files to your project. Later we'll talk about the many ways you can do that. Some of these methods use the position of the cursor to define where the new media file will be added. In this lesson, you'll learn how to reposition the cursor to establish the insertion point for adding new media.

pt **Private Tutor: Other reasons to reposition the cursor**

During your editing work, you'll constantly reposition the cursor to play back different portions of the project, perform edits, align various elements of the project, and more. The techniques you learn here will come in handy time after time as you assemble your Vegas projects.

To use the most common method of repositioning the cursor, click the timeline at the position where you want to move the cursor. To move the cursor to the beginning or end of the project, click the **Go To Start** or **Go To End** buttons on the transport controls shown in **Figure 2.4**.

Figure 2.4

You can quickly navigate to the beginning or end of your project.

Go to Start   Go to End   Cursor Position

Once you've clicked within the timeline, you can move the cursor with your keyboard. The **Right Arrow** and **Left Arrow** keys move the cursor to the right and left. By default, the cursor moves one screen pixel for each press of an arrow key. To move in larger intervals, Vegas uses the gray grid lines that run vertically through the timeline. Press **Page Up** to move to the previous grid line, or press **Page Down** to move to the next grid line.

You can also specify an exact time to which to move the cursor. Notice the three text boxes to the right of the navigation buttons shown in **Figure 2.4**. The **Cursor Position** box (on the left) updates whenever the cursor moves. You can also type a value into the **Cursor Position** box to move to that position. To enter a new value in the box, double-click the current value in the box or press **Ctrl + G** on your keyboard. This highlights the current value of the box. Type a new value and press **Enter**. The cursor jumps to the point in the project you specified.

Finally, click the **Play** button to play the project. When you get to the point in your project that you want to place the insertion point, click the **Pause** button. Vegas stops playback, and the cursor remains right where it is.

Task 5: Repositioning the project cursor

In this task, you'll reposition the cursor to define the insertion point for adding media to your project.

1. Navigate to the LessonFiles\Module2 folder, and open MO2Task005.veg.
2. Click the **Play** button.
3. After a few seconds, click the **Pause** button. Notice that the cursor stops and remains where it was when you clicked **Pause**.
4. Click the **Go To End** button to move the project cursor to the end of the project.
5. Press the **Page Up** key to jump the cursor to the previous grid mark.
6. Click in the timeline between the beginning of the project and the first grid mark.
7. Press **Ctrl + G** to select the value in the **Cursor Position** box. Type 0.12.6 and press Enter.

pt **Private tutor: The Video Preview window**

Notice that the Video Preview window always updates to reflect the project at the current cursor position. Watch the Video Preview window to find the exact point at which you want to place your insertion point.

Lesson 4: Adding media to your project

Once you've used the Explorer window to navigate to your media, previewed it to make sure it's what you want to use, and decided where in the timeline you want it to appear, you're ready to add the media to your project. This lesson presents several methods for adding media to your project. All of the techniques discussed here apply to adding media to audio and video tracks. Where differences exist, they are pointed out specifically.

One of the easiest ways to add a file to your project is to double-click the file in the Explorer window. Alternatively, select the file you want to add and press **Enter**. Either of these methods adds an event at the current cursor position. An event is a pointer to a media file: a video event displays thumbnail images of the video frames; an audio event displays the audio waveform.

pt Private Tutor: Determining the target track

You already learned that you can click a track icon to select that track. You can also click in the timeline to select a track. For instance, click Track 2 in the timeline of any project and observe that not only do you reposition your project cursor, but the track header is highlighted to indicate that Track 2 is selected. When you use either of the methods for adding a media file discussed above, the current cursor position and the currently selected track determine the destination of the file, so make sure you aim for the desired track when you click in the timeline to establish your insertion point.

pt Private Tutor: Understanding events

In order to fully master editing in Vegas, you must understand the concept of events. Events can be thought of as containers that hold media files. You can also think of an event as a window through which Vegas sees a media file. A single track can contain an unlimited number of events. The arrangement of events in the timeline determines the sequence of media files in your project. You'll learn all about working with events throughout the remainder of this book.

Task 6: Adding your first media files

In this task, you'll use the two basic techniques discussed above to add media files to a project.

1. Open *MO2Task006.veg* in the *\LessonFiles\Module02* folder on the companion CD. This project contains two empty video tracks and two empty audio tracks.
2. On Track 1 (a video track), click the first grid marker in the timeline to select Track 1 and place the cursor.
3. Navigate to the *\SampleMedia\Video* folder and double-click *eaglefly2.avi* to add it to the selected track at the cursor position. Vegas adds an event containing the video portion to the selected track and another event containing the audio portion of the file to the audio track directly below the target video track. (If there was not an audio track directly below the target video track, Vegas would create an audio track to hold the audio event.)
4. Click anywhere in Track 3 to select Track 3 and establish a new insertion point.
5. Navigate to the *\SampleMedia\Audio* folder and select *Dark Continent.wav* in the Explorer window.
6. Press **Enter** to add the selected file. Notice what happened. In Step 4, you selected a video track, and in Step 5 you added an audio file to your project. Since an audio event cannot reside on a video track, Vegas automatically added the file to a new event on the audio track directly below the selected track. (If there was not an audio track below the selected video track, Vegas would create one.)
7. Close the project without saving.

You can also use the simple drag-and-drop technique to add media to your project. To do this, drag the media file you want to use from the Explorer window to the timeline. Notice that when you drag the file over the correct track type (for instance, drag a video file over a video track), an outline of an event appears. Use this outline to guide you in the placement of the event. You can position the event anywhere on the timeline (in the appropriate track type) regardless of whether or not the track to which you drag the file is the currently selected track. When you've decided where you want the file to appear, position the event outline at that location, and release the mouse button. The event then appears on the target track.

Task 7: Adding files with the drag-and-drop method

In this task, you'll use the drag-and-drop technique to add media to your project.

1. Open *MO2Task007.veg* in the *\LessonFiles\Module02* folder on the companion CD. This project contains two empty tracks: one video and one audio.
2. Navigate to eaglefly2.avi in the \SampleMedia\Video folder.
3. Click *eaglefly2.avi*, and hold the mouse button down.
4. While still holding the mouse button, move the pointer to one of the empty tracks on the timeline. Notice that two event outlines appear, one over the video track, and one over the audio track.
5. Move the mouse back and forth to reposition the outlines on their respective tracks.
6. When you decide on a location for the event (anywhere toward the beginning of the timeline on the existing tracks will do just fine for this task), release the mouse button. The events now appear in the timeline.
7. Add *hawkMed.avi* to the timeline directly after the event you added in the previous steps.
8. Drag *eaglefly2.avi* to the project directly after the event that holds *hawkMed.avi*. Notice how quickly you can create a sequence of events with the drag-and-drop method. Notice also that the two tracks each contain three separate events, for a total of six events in your project. On each track, the first and third events hold exactly the same piece of media.
9. Close the project without saving.

Before we move on to a discussion of the next method for adding media to your project, let's talk for a moment about adding multiple files simultaneously. Vegas makes it easy to add multiple files to your project in one operation. You can use standard Windows techniques to select multiple files and follow the same procedures we've already discussed for adding them to your project (the double-click method discussed earlier does not work for multiple files).

Private Tutor: Standard Windows selection techniques

pt

You can use the **Ctrl** or the **Shift** keys to select multiple items. For instance, in the Explorer window, select a media file. Hold the **Ctrl** key and click another file. This adds the second file to the selection. In this way, you can add as many files as you want to the selection. Hold the **Ctrl** key and click a file that is already selected to remove the file from the selection.

Next, release the **Ctrl** key, and click the first file in the list. This selects the first file while deselecting any others. Now, hold the **Shift** key, and click the last file in the list. This adds the last file, and every other file between the first and the last, to the selection.

You can also click in an empty area within the Explorer list view and drag a selection rectangle. When you release the mouse button, all of the files within the rectangle are selected.

Task 8: Adding multiple files simultaneously

In this task, you'll employ two of the methods you already know for adding files to your project to add multiple files at the same time.

1. Open the Vegas project *MO2Task008.veg* in the *LessonFiles\Module02* folder on the companion CD. This project contains two empty tracks, one video and one audio.
2. Click in the timeline to place the cursor.
3. Select eaglefly2.avi in the SampleMedia\Video folder.
4. Hold the **Shift** key on your keyboard and click *hawkMed.avi*. This adds *hawkMed.avi*, *fireweed.avi*, and *grizzlywalks.avi* to the selection. You now have all four of these files selected simultaneously in the Explorer window.
5. Press the **Enter** key. Vegas adds the four files to the timeline, one after the other, in the order in which they appear in the Explorer window list.
6. With all four files still selected in the Explorer window, drag *hawkMed.avi* to the existing tracks on the timeline. Again, this adds all four files to the tracks, but notice the order. The *hawkMed.avi* event appears before the other three in the timeline, even though it appears after them in the Explorer window list. This illustrates that when you use the drag-and-drop method to add multiple files, the file you drag appears first in the timeline. Remaining files appear according to their order in the Explorer window.
7. Close this project without saving your changes.

Normally, when you add multiple files simultaneously, Vegas automatically positions the events so that they appear end to end on the same track. However, you can also add multiple files so that the edges overlap and create automatic crossfades. Choose **Options | Preferences** to open the Preferences dialog, and click the **Editing** tab. Use the **Automatically overlap multiple selected media when added** check box in conjunction with the **Amount (seconds)** settings in the **Cut-to-overlap conversion** section to modify the default behavior so the files overlap one another. When Vegas is in Automatic Crossfades mode (which it is by default), overlapping events creates a crossfade from the first event to next.

pt Private Tutor: Crossfades

We'll talk more about crossfades later, but here's a simple definition: a crossfade occurs when two events overlap, and the first event fades out (disappears gradually over a given period of time) while the second event fades in (appears gradually over the same period of time).

Task 9: Automatically overlapping multiple events

In this task, you'll change the Vegas default settings in order to create automatic crossfades when you add multiple events to your project.

1. Choose **Options | Preferences** to open the Preferences dialog, and click the **Editing** tab.
2. Select the **Automatically overlap multiple selected media when added** check box.
3. Double-click the **Amount (seconds)** box to select the current value.
4. Type "3.0" in the box and click the **OK** button.
5. Select eaglefly2.avi, hawkMed.avi, and grizzlywalks.avi in the Explorer window.
6. Drag *eaglefly2.avi* into the existing tracks of the timeline. Notice that the events now overlap by three seconds as indicated by the "X" between the events.
7. Click the **Play** button and notice that when the cursor reaches the crossfaded area between two events, the first event fades out while the second fades in.
8. You can also access the Preferences dialog directly from the track list or the timeline. Right-click a blank spot in either area (do not click within an existing track

or track header), and choose **Preferences** from the shortcut menu. Click the
Editing tab.

9. Click the **Default All** button to restore the Vegas Editing preferences to their
    default settings.
10. Close the project without saving your changes.

Think of the next method for adding media to your project as a set of extensions to the drag-and-drop method we
discussed earlier. These extensions offer several useful commands for exactly how you want to add your files. To
access these commands, use the right mouse button to drag a file (or files) to the timeline. When you release the
button, a shortcut menu displays several commands.

For now, note the three commands at the top of the shortcut menu:

- **Add Across Time**
- **Add Across Tracks**
- **Add As Takes**

Before we discuss each of these in detail, notice that the second section of the shortcut menu contains two
commands: **Video Only** and **Audio Only**. You saw earlier that when you added a video file to your project, the video
was added to a video track, and the audio was added to an audio track. The Video Only and Audio Only commands
enable you to use only the portion of the file you need.

For instance, perhaps you have a video file with usable video but unusable audio. In such a case, choose one of the
Video Only options, and Vegas adds just the video portion to your project. Thus, you can skip the step of deleting the
audio after you add the file. You can then proceed to add more appropriate audio.

Hover your mouse over the **Video Only** and **Audio Only** commands, and notice that a submenu appears. The
submenu contains the same three commands mentioned above. Let's talk about those commands now.

The first two commands only have an effect when you add multiple files. The **Add Across Time** command behaves
much the same as the procedures we discussed earlier for adding multiple files. All of the selected files are added to
the target track one after the other. The **Add Across Tracks** command adds each file to a separate track. If your
project does not contain enough tracks to hold all of the files, Vegas adds new tracks.

Task 10: Adding media files across time

In this task, you'll add the video portions of three media files across time on the same track.

1. Follow Steps 1 through 4 in Task 8 to select four video files (eaglefly.avi,
    fireweed.avi, grizzlywalks.avi, and hawkMed.avi).
2. Right-click and drag the files to the video track in the timeline. Remember that the
    file you drag appears as the first file in the sequence.
3. Release the mouse button, and choose **Video Only | Add Video Across Time**
    from the shortcut menu. Four events appear one after the other in the video track
    containing the video portions of each file. The audio track remains empty since you
    did not add the audio.

Task 11: Adding media files across tracks

In this task, you'll add just the video portions of three media files across tracks.

1. Follow Steps 1 through 3 in *Task 8* to select four video files.
2. Right-click and drag the files to the video track in the timeline. Remember that the
    file you drag appears as the first file in the sequence.
3. Release the mouse button, and choose **Video Only | Add Video Across Tracks**
    from the shortcut menu. Notice that the first clip appears on Track 1. Track 2 (the
    audio track) is empty since you added video only. Three new tracks (Tracks 3, 4, and
    5) have been added to your project to hold the remaining video files. Notice that all
    of the events start at the same point in the timeline.

The **Add As Takes** option allows you to add more than one media file to a single event. This is very useful for making multiple versions of the same video. For instance, perhaps you are editing a 30-second commercial that tells your customers where they can buy a product. You need one version for "The Art Shop" in Chicago and another for "Art's Arts Cart" in Los Angeles. In this case, add both versions to the same event as separate takes. Takes allow you to quickly switch between different versions of the video or audio recording.

On an event that holds more than one take, right-click the event and choose **Take** from the shortcut menu. A submenu appears with a number of commands. The bottom section of the submenu lists all of the takes available for the event. Select a name from the list to make that clip the active take. The thumbnail in the event reflects the active take. In an audio event, the waveform for the active take appears in the event.

To scroll through the takes in an event, choose **Next Take** or **Previous Take** from the submenu. Alternately, click the event, and press **T** for the next take or **Shift+T** for the previous take.

To remove the active take from an event, choose **Delete Active** from the submenu. To delete a take other than the active take, choose **Delete** from the submenu to open the Delete Takes dialog. Click the name of the take you want to remove. Click the **Play** button (in the Delete Takes dialog) to preview the take and confirm that you have selected the correct take. Click **OK** to delete the selected take. Deleting a take does not delete the file from your hard drive. It simply deletes the take from the event.

Task 12: Working with multiple takes

In this task, you'll add just the video portions of three media files as takes to one event and then perform various operations on those takes.

1. Open *MO2Task008.veg* in the *LessonFiles\Module02* folder on the companion CD..
2. Navigate to the \SampleMedia\Video folder, and select eaglefly2.avi, grizzlywalks.avi, and hawkMed.avi.
3. Right-click and drag *grizzlywalks.avi* to the video track in the timeline. (The file you drag defines the length of the event.)
4. Release the mouse button and choose **Video Only | Add Video As Takes** from the shortcut menu. Vegas adds one event to the timeline. This event holds all three media files as separate takes.
5. Right-click the event and choose **Take** | *eaglefly2* from the list at the bottom of the shortcut menu. The event thumbnail now shows *eaglefly2* (now the active take).
6. Press **T** to make *grizzlywalks* the active take.
7. Close the project without saving your changes.

pt **Private Tutor: Adding takes to an existing event**

You can also add files as alternate takes to an event that already exists in the timeline. Use the same right-click procedure for adding the files to the timeline, but make sure to drop the files directly onto the event to which you want to add the multiple takes. Choose **Add As Takes** from the shortcut menu. The event now contains multiple takes.

pt **Private Tutor: A shortcut for adding multiple files**

You can drag multiple files to the timeline with the left mouse button, then (while still holding the left mouse button) click the right mouse button to toggle through the three commands that appear in the shortcut menu. As you toggle through the commands, you'll notice that the outline changes to reflect the currently selected option.

So far we've talked mostly about adding video and audio files. As mentioned earlier, Vegas also supports a number of still image file formats. For the most part, you use the same techniques discussed above to add still image files.

However, when you add a video file, the length of the media dictates the length of the event. For instance, if you add a video clip that lasts for 3.5 seconds, Vegas creates a 3.5-second event to hold it. In contrast, still images have no intrinsic length, so Vegas chooses a length for you.

You can change the default length for your still images in the Editing tab of the Preferences dialog. To do so, change the value in the **New still image length (seconds)** box.

Task 13: Adding still images to your project

In this task, you'll add still images to your project and change the default length of new still images.

1. Open *MO2Task008.veg* in the *LessonFiles\Module02* folder on the companion CD..
2. Navigate to the *SampleMedia\StillImages* folder on the CD-ROM.
3. Select *Abraham Lincoln.jpg* and click the **Start Preview** button to preview the file before you add it to your project.
4. Use any of the techniques you learned earlier to add the file to your project. Vegas creates an event to hold the image that lasts for the default length.
5. Choose **Options | Preferences**, and in the Preferences dialog, click the **Editing** tab.
6. Double-click the **New still image length (seconds)** box to highlight the current value.
7. Type "10.0" to make the default length of still images 10 seconds. Click **OK** to close the Preferences dialog and apply the change.
8. Add *White House.jpg* to your project.
9. Open the Editing tab of the Preferences dialog again.
10. Click the **Default All** button to restore the Vegas defaults.
11. Close the project without saving your changes.

pt
Private Tutor: Alpha channel support

Some still image formats support an alpha channel or transparent layer or color. Vegas supports this image information, so you can freely utilize the alpha channel and transparency for creating overlays and titles in your Vegas projects.

Lesson 5: Creating and deleting tracks

So far, most of the media you've added to your projects has been added to existing tracks. In reality, every new project contains no tracks, so you'll have to add tracks to hold your events. As your projects become more complex, you'll use many tracks. In this lesson, you'll learn the many ways to add new tracks to hold media. You'll also learn how to delete tracks that you no longer need.

The Insert menu provides the most basic method for adding new tracks. Choose **Insert | Audio Track** or **Insert | Video Track**. With this method, the new audio track always becomes the last track in your project, and the new video track always becomes Track 1.

Task 14: Adding new tracks from the Insert menu

In this task, you'll use the Insert menu to add new tracks to a blank project.

1. Click the **New** button to start a new Vegas project.
2. Choose **Insert | Video Track** to add a video track to the project (or press **Shift+Ctrl+Q**).
3. In the same way, add an audio track (the keyboard shortcut is **Ctrl+Q**). Notice that the audio track appears at the bottom of the track list.
4. Make note of the color of the track icon for Track 1. Repeat Steps 1 and 2. You can see by the color of the track icons that the new video track was added as the first track in the project.
5. Make note of the color of the track icon for the audio track. Insert another audio track. The track icon colors show that the new track was added as the last track in the project.

pt Private Tutor: Starting a new project

In the previous task, you used the **New** button to start a new project. You also could have chosen **File | New** to start your new project. However, when you start a new project with **File | New**, Vegas opens the New Project dialog. There are many options and settings in the New Project dialog, some of which are quite complex. The New Project dialog is exactly the same as the Project Properties dialog. Take some time to explore the Project Properties dialog, and consult the help files and .pdf manual for more information.

The track list area and the timeline also provide tools for adding new tracks. Right-click a blank area in the track list or the timeline. The shortcut menu contains commands to insert tracks, and these commands achieve the same results as adding tracks through the Insert menu.

Track headers allow you to add tracks and achieve slightly different results. Right-click any track icon. A command in the shortcut menu enables you to add a track of the same type as the track you right-clicked. For instance, right-click the track icon for a video track, and choose **Insert Video Track** to add a new video track. On an audio track, the command is **Insert Audio Track**. Tracks added with this method do not follow the same ordering rules as those discussed earlier. Tracks added from the track header shortcut menu always appear directly above the track you right-clicked. This can be a valuable tool when your project contains more tracks than can fit on your screen at one time because the new track appears close to where you were already looking.

Task 15: Adding new tracks from track headers

In this task, you'll use the track header to add new tracks. You'll learn how the results differ from the method you used in the previous task.

1. Click the **New** button to start a new Vegas project. Click **No** if you are asked if you want to save changes to the current project.
2. Right-click the track list area and choose **Insert Audio Track** from the shortcut menu.
3. Right-click a blank area of the timeline (aim for the dark gray area, not within the light gray of the new track you added in step 2), and choose **Insert Video Track** from the shortcut menu.
4. Use any method to add another video track.
5. Right-click the track icon for the audio track (track 3). Choose **Insert Audio Track**. Recall that with the methods you learned earlier, an audio track is added at the bottom of the track list. But with this method, the new track appears directly above the track you clicked.
6. Right-click the track icon for Track 2 and choose **Insert Video Track** from the shortcut menu. Recall that so far new video tracks have always appeared as the first track in the track list. As you saw in Step 5, with this method, the new track appears directly above the track you clicked.

You can also duplicate an existing track in order to create a new one. This technique creates an exact duplicate of the existing track, meaning that any events on the original track also appear on the duplicate track. To duplicate a track, right-click its track icon and choose **Duplicate Track** from the shortcut menu. The duplicate track appears directly below the original track.

Task 16: Duplicating a track

In this task, you'll learn how to make a duplicate of an existing track. You'll see that all of the events and settings of the original track also appear on the duplicate track.

1. Open *MO2Task016.veg* in the *LessonFiles\Module02* folder on the companion CD-ROM.
2. Right-click the track icon for the existing track and choose **Duplicate Track** from the shortcut menu. You now have two identical tracks in your project.

pt **Private Tutor: Modifying the duplicate track**

In Task 16, *Duplicating a track*, you used the **Duplicate Track** command to make an exact copy of an existing track. Even though the two tracks are identical, they are independent of one another. You can change either of the tracks and the events on them without affecting the other. Using techniques that you'll learn in later lessons, you can use this independence to create interesting special effects.

If you do not have enough tracks in your project to hold all of the media files you are trying to add across tracks, Vegas creates the tracks you need. Similarly, you can drag a file from the Explorer window to a blank area of either the track list or the track view (timeline). Since you have not dropped the file into an existing track, Vegas creates a new track to hold it. We sometimes refer to this method as adding a new track on the fly.

Many times you'll actually want to delete an existing track. To do so, right-click a track icon and choose **Delete** from the shortcut menu. Alternatively, right-click a blank spot in the timeline for the track and choose **Delete** from the shortcut menu. Finally, click the track icon for the track you want to remove and press the **Delete** key. Of course, when you delete a track, you also remove all events on that track.

Task 17: Adding a new track on the fly

In this task, you'll learn how to add a new track to your project while simultaneously adding a media file to the timeline. Along the way, you'll also learn how to delete a track that you no longer need. You'll see that the results you achieve depend upon the current configuration of your project and exactly where you drop the new file.

1. Open *MO2Task016.veg* from the *\LessonFiles\Module02* folder on the companion CD-ROM.

2. Navigate to the *\SampleMedia\Video* folder.

3. Right-click and drag *hawkMed.avi* to a blank spot in the existing track. From the shortcut menu, choose **Video Only | Add Video Across Time**. Since you dropped the file onto an existing track and you did not add the audio, Vegas does not create a new track.

4. Right-click and drag *eaglefly2.avi* to a blank area in the timeline (not within the existing track). From the shortcut menu, choose **Video Only | Add Video Across Time**. This time, since you did not drop the file onto an existing track, Vegas creates a new track to hold the new event. Notice that the new track appears below the existing track.

5. Now add both the video and audio portions of a file. Drag *grizzlywalks.avi* to a blank space on Track 2. Vegas adds the video portion of the clip to the existing video track, but since no audio track exists, Vegas adds one to your project to hold the audio portion of the media file.

6. Drag *hawkMed.avi* to a blank space in Track 1. The video portion of the file appears on Track 1, but since there was no audio track directly below Track 1, Vegas created a new one to hold the audio. If there had been an audio track directly below the video track, no new track would have been created.

7. You're accumulating a number of tracks, so let's remove a few. Right-click the track icon for Track 2. Choose **Delete** from the shortcut menu.

8. Notice that the new Track 2 is selected. Press the **Delete** key to delete it. Press the **Delete** key again to remove one more track.

9. Drag *grizzlywalks.avi* to a blank spot on the timeline. Vegas creates two new tracks to hold the file: one for the video and one for the audio.

Conclusion

You learned a lot in this module. You now know all about the Explorer window and how to use it to navigate to, preview, and add media files to your project. You can now easily define the exact point in your project at which you want to add your media, and add that media using any of several methods. Finally, you learned how to add and delete tracks. By now you realize that Vegas is extremely flexible in that it gives you many different ways to accomplish a task. As you work more and more with Vegas, most of what you learned by completing the tasks in these lessons will become second nature to you.

Exercises

1. The Explorer Window in Vegas works very much like Windows Explorer. What then is the major advantage to using the Explorer window to navigate to your files?

    a. The Explorer window is faster.

    b. The Explorer window allows you to change the names of your files.

    c. The Explorer window allows you to quickly preview your media files.

    d. The Explorer window uses less of your computer's RAM.

2. True or false: Changes you make to your files in the Explorer window (such as deleting or renaming files) have the same effect as making those changes in Windows Explorer.

3. Which of the following are ways to preview a media file in the Explorer window?

    a. Select the file and click the **Preview File Now** button.

    b. Select the file and click the **Start Preview** button.

    c. Drag the file from the Explorer window to the Video Preview window.

    d. Click the **Auto Preview** button then select the file.

4. True or false: Although Vegas supports many file formats, .avi is the only video format that you can preview before adding a file to the project.

5. True or false: Vegas supports many video, audio, and still image formats, and it's easy to use any of these formats in the same project without doing anything special to prepare the files before adding them to your project.

6. Which of the following is a legitimate method of placing the cursor in your timeline in preparation for adding media to your project? Choose all that apply.

    a. Click the **Go To Start** button.

    b. Click in the timeline at the point where you want to position the cursor.

    c. Type a specific value into the **Cursor Position** box.

    d. Click in the timeline, then press the **Page Up** or **Page Down** button on your keyboard.

7. Which phrase below best defines an *event* in Vegas

    a. The result of clicking one of the interface buttons.

    b. The video that appears in the Video Preview window when you play your project.

    c. A container in the timeline that can hold one or more media files.

    d. The process of navigating to, previewing, and adding a file to your project.

8. True or false: When using the drag-and-drop method to add multiple files to the timeline, the file you drag is added to the timeline before all the other files you've selected and the remaining files appear in the order in which they appear in the Explorer window.

9. Which of the following is **not** a valid option when using the right-click-and-drag method for adding multiple files?

   a. Add Across Tracks

   b. Add as Takes

   c. Add as Overlapped Events

   d. Add Across Time

10. True or false: Before you can add a clip to the timeline, you must always add a new track to your project to hold it.

11. Which of the following is a handy way to make an exact copy of an existing track?

    a. Select the track, choose **File | Copy**, and then choose **File | Paste**.

    b. Right-click the track header and choose **Clone Track** from the shortcut menu.

    c. Select the track and press **Ctrl+D**.

    d. Right-click the track header and choose **Duplicate** from the shortcut menu.

12. Draw a line connecting the keyboard shortcut to the action it performs:

    a. Ctrl+G   Add a file to the current selection.

    b. Right Arrow   Select the previous take in an event with multiple takes.

    c. Ctrl+Click   Move the timeline cursor to the right.

    d. Shift+T   Highlight the value in the **Current Cursor Position** field.

    e. Shift+Ctrl+Q   Insert a new video track.

Essays

1. Briefly explain the term *crossfade*.

2. Describe the fundamental difference in the results achieved between adding a new track through the Insert menu as opposed to adding a new track through an existing track's right-click shortcut menu.

3. Describe how you add files as multiple takes. Discuss a scenario in which it would be helpful to add several media files as multiple takes of one event in the timeline.

Module 3: Adding media to your project—advanced methods

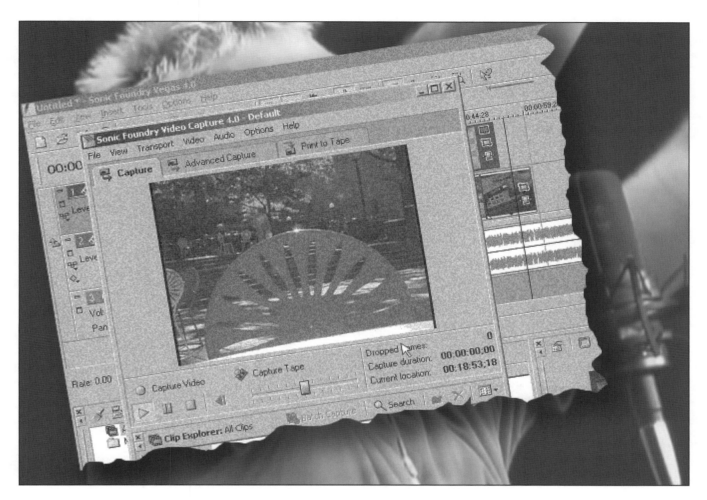

Module 2 showed you how to add existing media to your project, but sometimes you want to create your own media. For instance, you may want to add video you shot with your camcorder or add your voice as narration. This module shows you how to get video from your camera to your computer, how to record audio, and how to extract audio from your CD collection for use in your projects. Once you've captured video or recorded/extracted audio, you can work with it just like any other file you use in Vegas.

In this module you'll do the following:

- Learn what hardware you need for capturing video.
- Capture video that you can use in your projects.
- Learn how to set up a basic audio recording system.
- Record audio into your Vegas project.
- Extract audio from an audio CD.
- Add the media that you create into a project.

Lesson 1: Capturing video

The real fun (and usefulness) of Vegas comes when you start editing video that you shoot with your own video camera. But how do you get the video from the camera to your computer? That's what this lesson teaches you.

> **Private Tutor: Learning about the technology of digital video**
>
> *pt* Much of the discussion below relating to the hardware required to capture video may be completely new to you. If so, we suggest you visit http://www.consumerdvreviews.com/editing/getstart.asp for a good beginner's discussion on the technology involved.

Vegas has been built to work seamlessly with your digital video (DV) camcorder. Use an IEEE-1394 cable to connect your DV camcorder to an OHCI-compliant IEEE-1394 (commonly known as FireWire) card installed in your computer (usually in an available PCI slot, but often built into the computer). If you've purchased an OHCI-compliant video capture card, Vegas (and the video capture application that we'll talk about in a moment) can communicate with your DV camcorder via the FireWire connection so you can control the camera (play, stop, rewind and so on) from your computer.

Task 1: Connecting your DV camcorder to your computer

In this task you'll connect your camcorder to your computer's FireWire video capture card.

1. Make sure your computer has a properly installed FireWire video capture card.
2. Connect your DV camcorder to your capture card with FireWire cable.

> **Private Tutor: Capturing video from an analog camcorder**
>
> *pt* We limit this discussion to DV because DV technology plays to the strengths of Vegas. However, you don't have to shoot your video on a DV camcorder. There are many analog video capture cards available (cards that turn analog video output from your camcorder into digital video on your computer). However, be aware that you may not be able to control your video camera using the video capture utility described here when you use an analog capture card. Another method of capturing analog video is to use an external analog-to-DV converter.

When you installed Vegas, the Sonic Foundry Video Capture utility was automatically installed. To specify a different video capture application, choose **Options | Preferences**, click the **Video** tab in the Preferences dialog, and click the **Browse** button next to the **Preferred video capture application** box. Then browse to your desired application and click **OK** to close the Preferences dialog.

To prepare to capture video from your DV camcorder, connect your camcorder to your PC (as discussed above) and turn it on in VCR or VTR mode. Choose **File | Capture Video**. This starts the Sonic Foundry Video Capture utility (assuming you have not changed your preferred application as discussed above) with the **Capture** tab active.

The **Verify Tape Name** dialog appears (this dialog may not appear if you do not have a DV camcorder or tape deck connected to your computer). Here you can assign a name to the tape from which you are capturing video or choose a name from the list. The tape name is embedded in the file that is created during the capture process. You can leave this box blank, but naming each tape helps you keep your tapes organized and find clips that you used in old projects. You have three options on how to proceed:

- Select the **Don't capture any clips right now** radio button to capture only a portion of the tape.
- Select the **Start capturing all clips from the current tape position** radio to capture everything on the tape from the current position.
- Select **Start capturing all clips from the beginning of the tape** to automatically rewind the tape to the beginning and then capture the entire tape.

After you make your choice, click **OK**. If you choose the second or third option, Video Capture begins playback of your DV camcorder or tape deck and starts capturing video from your tape. If you choose the first option, Video Capture waits for further instructions from you. The video display area says "Device Stopped."

Task 2: Getting ready to capture video

This task shows you how to open the Sonic Foundry Video Capture utility.

1. Click the **New** button to start a new Vegas project.
2. Set your DV camcorder to VCR or VTR mode.
3. Insert the DV tape from which you want to capture video into your DV camcorder or tape deck.
4. Choose **File | Capture Video**.
5. Leave the **Tape Name** box blank, and select **Don't capture any clips right now** in the Verify Tape Name dialog, and click **OK**.

Use the transport controls, as shown in **Figure 3.1**, to preview your tape and find the exact spot where you want to begin capturing video. Remember that the transport buttons control the playback of the tape in your DV device. The **Play**, **Pause**, and **Stop** buttons work the same as the physical buttons on your camcorder. Click the **Step Backward** or **Step Forward** button to move the tape backward or forward one video frame. Click the **Rewind** (Shift+Left Arrow) or **Fast Forward** (Shift+Right Arrow) button to rewind or fast-forward the tape to the desired position. Drag the **Shuttle** slider in either direction to view the tape at various speeds. The farther away from the center point you drag the slider, the faster the video plays back.

Figure 3.1

The buttons in the Video Capture transport bar give you various options for capturing video.

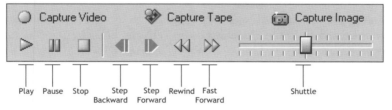

Play Pause Stop Step Backward Step Forward Rewind Fast Forward Shuttle

Private Tutor: Capturing heads and tails

In Module 6, *Basic Editing Techniques* you'll learn to trim the beginnings and ends of your events. You can use those techniques to trim unwanted material from the beginning and end of your captured clips too, so you don't have to worry about capturing exactly what you think you'll use. We suggest you start capturing a few seconds before the material you think you'll use starts (known as capturing a "head") and stop capturing a few seconds after the desired material ends (known as capturing a "tail"). Remember, it's a lot easier to trim the head and tail if you don't need them than it is to recapture the clip if you didn't capture enough the first time.

Figure 3.1 also shows the various buttons used in the capture process. To automatically rewind the tape to the beginning and then capture the entire tape, click the **Capture Tape** button. To begin capturing at the current tape position, click the **Capture Video** button (**Ctrl+R**). Video Capture begins playback of the tape on your camera and simultaneously captures the video to your computer. Click the **Capture Image** button (**Ctrl+Shift+R**) to capture a still image of the current frame.

When you've captured your footage, click the **Stop** button in the transport bar. The Capture Complete dialog displays information about the video you just captured. Select the **Add captured clips to the Media Pool** check box. Click the **Show Clips** button to view thumbnails of the clips you captured.

> ### *pt* Private Tutor: Smart capture
> You may have captured several clips even though you only clicked the **Capture Video** or **Capture Tape** button once. Video Capture has several ways to detect new scenes. For instance, a new scene is detected every time you turned the camera off and then back on in record mode. Each of these scenes is captured as a separate video file.

Click the **Rename All** button to open the Rename All dialog. Type a name in the **Base name for clips** box. This name is used as a prefix to the clip number that can help you organize your clips later. Click **OK**. To rename a single clip, right-click the thumbnail and choose **Rename** from the shortcut menu.

If you decide that you don't want these clips after all, click the **Delete All** button to remove them from your hard drive. To delete a single clip, right-click the thumbnail and choose **Delete** from the shortcut menu.

Click the **Done** button to close the Capture Complete dialog. The **Save As** dialog opens to give you the opportunity to save this video capture session. Saving a session allows you to reopen it and work further with it later. Usually, you don't need to save the session, so click the **Cancel** button. The captured clips appear in the Clip Explorer area at the bottom of the Video Capture window. Click the **Close** button at the top-right corner of the Video Capture window. You may be asked again if you want to save the session. Click **Yes** if you do, or click **No** if you don't.

Task 3: Capturing video

In this task you'll capture video from your DV camcorder or tape deck to your computer.

1. Click the **Play** button in the Video Capture transport bar to begin playback of the tape.
2. When you reach the point in the tape where you want to start capturing, click the **Pause** button to suspend playback.
3. If you didn't pause the tape at the exact spot where you want to begin capturing, use the **Step Backward** and **Step Forward** buttons or the **Shuttle** slider to adjust the start position.
4. Click the **Capture Video** button to begin capturing.
5. When you reach the end of the material you want to capture, click the **Stop** button.
6. In the Capture Complete dialog, click the **Show Clips** button if the thumbnails are not visible.
7. Select the **Add captured clips to the Media Pool** check box if it is not already selected.
8. Click the **Rename All** button to open the Rename All dialog.
9. Select the current text in the **Base name for clips** field, type "Learn2Capture" and click the **OK** button.
10. Click the **Done** button.
11. Click the **Cancel** button to skip saving the capture session.
12. Click the **Close** button to close the Sonic Foundry Video Capture window. Click **No** if asked if you want to save your changes.

After you closed the Sonic Foundry Video Capture window in the last task, you were taken back to Vegas. In the window docking area, the **Media Pool** has been brought forward, and it already contains the files that you just captured (it may also contain other files that you have already added to your project).

Private Tutor: Introducing the Media Pool

pt The Media Pool helps you organize all of the assets (media files) of your Vegas project. When you add a clip to the timeline or capture video using Sonic Foundry Video Capture, Vegas creates a reference to that file in the Media Pool. You can create bins to organize media clips into logically related groups. Bins help you organize your media and easily search for related clips using, keywords, file types, frame rates, and other media properties. If you decide to add the media to your project again (or possibly for the first time with captured files), you can use the Media Pool instead of the Explorer window to quickly find the media that you want.

As shown in **Figure 3.2**, the Media Pool includes the same preview buttons you used in the Explorer window. You can preview your clips and then use the techniques you learned with the Explorer window to add clips to the timeline right from the Media Pool.

Figure 3.2
The Media Pool gives you another easy way to preview and add files to your project.
You access many other functions from the Media Pool also

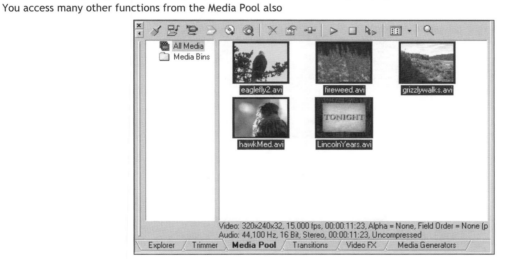

Task 4: Adding clips from the Media Pool

In this task you'll add a media file to your timeline directly from the Media Pool.

1. In the Media Pool, select one of the clips you just captured.
2. Click the **Start Preview** button to view the clip in the Video Preview window.
3. Drag the clip from the Media Pool to the timeline.
4. Position your cursor at the beginning of the event and click the **Play** button in the Vegas transport bar to view your captured clip in the timeline.

Now that you've captured your video and added it to the timeline, you can combine it with any other media to create your movie.

Lesson 2: Recording audio

In the previous lesson, you learned how to capture video from your DV camcorder. As you would expect, this process also added the audio associated with the captured video to your project. That's one way to add original audio to your project. You can also record audio directly into an audio track. In this lesson you'll learn to record audio into Vegas.

pt **Private Tutor: Turning off the Input Monitoring feature**

You can monitor the input signal through your sound card while setting audio levels and recording. This handy feature is useful mostly in advanced recording setups. You will not need it for any of the following tasks since we talk about very basic techniques here. You may experience feedback (an unpleasant squealing noise from your computer speakers) while working through some of the tasks in this section with input monitoring active. Therefore, we recommend you turn input monitoring off. Right-click the track icon in the track header of your audio track. Choose **Record Inputs | Input Monitor** as shown in **Figure 3.3**. This turns off input monitoring.

Figure 3.3
A check mark before the **Input Monitor** command indicates that input monitoring is active. Choose the option to deactivate the feature.

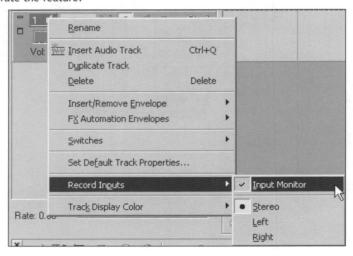

pt **Private Tutor: Setting the default track properties**

You can customize several properties of a track and then save those settings as the default so that all new tracks start with those track properties. For example, you can turn off input monitoring on one track (as in the previous Private Tutor) and then set that as the default for all new audio tracks. To set your default track properties so input monitoring is off, first turn it off for an audio track. Then, right-click that track's track icon and choose **Set Default Track Properties**. In the Set Default Track Properties dialog, select the **Input Monitor** check box (if it is not already selected). Click **OK**. This turns input monitoring off by default for all new tracks in this project and in all of your projects. Take a moment to study the other track properties that can be set as defaults using this method.

As with capturing video, you'll need to make sure you have the proper hardware before you begin. In the most basic setup, you'll have an audio input device (normally a microphone or an electronic device such as an electric piano or a tape deck) connected to the inputs of your computer sound card. In a slightly more complex setup, you might connect your audio device to a mixing console (mixer) and connect the mixer to the sound card in your computer.

pt Private Tutor: Matching input devices to sound card inputs

Many computer sound cards have two types of input jacks: microphone-level (Mic) and line-level (Line-In). Almost without exception, you'll only connect to the Mic input when you plug a microphone directly into the sound card. Because the typical microphone sends a relatively weak signal, the microphone input on your sound card boosts the signal. Because line-level devices (electronic keyboards, tape decks, and mixers) send a stronger signal, the extra boost isn't needed. Therefore, line inputs on your sound card provide no extra amplification. If you connect a microphone to a line input, the signal will likely be too weak to be usable. Conversely, if you connect a line device to a microphone input, the resulting signal will be too strong and may cause an unpleasant sound known as distortion, and could even damage the input circuitry. However, if you first connect a microphone to a mixer, you'll typically connect the mixer to a line input on the sound card since the mixer provides the amplification that the microphone needs, then outputs a line-level audio signal.

pt Private Tutor: Making the connection

Many computer sound cards use 1/8-inch mini plug connections. Electronic keyboards usually use a 1/4-inch connector, tape decks normally use RCA or phono connectors, and microphones often use yet another type of connector, called XLR. You might need an adapter to properly connect your audio device to your computer's sound input.

Task 5: Connecting a microphone to your computer

In this task you'll connect a microphone to the sound card in your computer.

1. Compare the connector on the end of your microphone to the microphone input on your sound card. If the microphone connector does not match the mic-in jack, find an adapter to convert the microphone plug.
2. Plug the microphone into the microphone input jack on your computer sound card.

After you connect the audio device, you need to establish proper recording levels. To do this, you'll have to step out of Vegas for a moment and use the Windows Recording Control or the recording control software that came with your sound card. We'll talk about the Windows Recording Control here; if your sound card has its own recording controls, check the sound card's documentation to learn how to set your recording levels.

The Windows Recording Control determines the audio level sent to Vegas during recording. In Windows, choose **Start | Programs | Accessories | Entertainment | Volume Control** (or double-click the speaker icon in the Windows system tray) to open the Windows Mixer.

In the Windows Volume control, choose **Options | Properties** to open the Properties dialog. In the Properties dialog, choose the desired sound card from the **Mixer Device** drop-down list.

Private Tutor: Choosing the sound card input

pt　Typically, a computer has only one sound card. But some computers have multiple sound cards. Other computers have one sound card that has more than one input jack. If you have multiple sound cards or multiple inputs, choose the desired card or input from the **Mixer device** drop-down.

Select the **Recording** radio button in the **Adjust volume for** section. Select **Line** and/or **Microphone** from the **Show the following volume controls** list. Click **OK**. The Record Control, shown in **Figure 3.4**, opens with faders for Line and/or Microphone. Select **Microphone** as the active input. Leave the Record Control open because you'll use these controls in a few minutes to adjust the recording level of your input device. You might want to resize Vegas so that you can see Vegas and the Record Control on your computer screen simultaneously.

Figure 3.4
Use the Windows Record Control to set the record input level in Vegas.

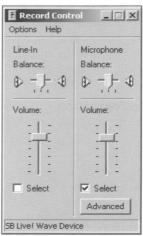

Back in Vegas, choose **Insert | Audio Track** to add a new audio track to your project. In the track header for the new track, click the **Arm for Record** button, shown in **Figure 3.5**. The **Project Recorded Files Folder** dialog appears. Here you specify or browse to the folder on your computer where you want to store the audio file you are about to create. Once you've specified the recorded files path, click **OK** to close the dialog.

Figure 3.5
Click the **Arm for Record** button to prepare the track for recording.

Arm for Record

In the track header, the **Volume** and **Pan** faders disappear and are replaced by an audio meter. This meter helps you monitor the recording level so that you can set it properly. Send a signal to your sound card input (that is, talk into the microphone, play your tape, or play your electronic keyboard). While watching the meter react to the signal, adjust the appropriate volume control in the Windows Record Control to adjust the signal as necessary.

Private Tutor: Setting proper recording levels

pt

A number appears at the right end of the track's recording meter. This number indicates the highest level (or peak) reached by the meter as it receives signal. To achieve a good recording level, make certain that this number falls somewhere between –6 dB and –3 dB. Anything below –6 could be too weak to provide a good recording, and anything over –3 dB can result in distortion of the audio. If the number is displayed in a red box, the signal has clipped, and the recording level should be brought down. To reset the number so that you can see what the new peak is (after adjusting the Record Control), click the number.

Task 6: Preparing to record with a microphone

This task shows you how to get ready to record using a microphone.

1. In Windows, choose **Start | Programs | Accessories | Entertainment | Volume Control**.
2. Choose **Options | Properties**.
3. In the Properties dialog, choose the desired device from the **Mixer device** drop-down list.
4. Click the **Recording** radio button in the **Adjust volume for** section.
5. Select **Microphone** from the **Show the following volume controls** list.
6. Click **OK**
7. Select **Microphone** as the active input.
8. Position or resize the Vegas window so that you can see the Record Control while working in Vegas.
9. In a new Vegas project, insert an audio track.
10. Click the **Arm for Record** button for the new track.
11. Click the **Browse** button in the Project Recorded Files Folder dialog.
12. In the **Browse For Folder** dialog, navigate to the *My Documents* folder.
13. Click the **New Folder** button. Name the new folder *VegasRecord*. Click the **OK** button.
14. Click the **OK** button in the Recorded Files Folder dialog.
15. Speak into the microphone, and use the Windows Record Control to adjust the input level until it peaks between –6 dB and –3 dB.

With your input device properly connected, your record path specified, and your recording levels properly set, click the **Record** button in the Vegas transport bar (or press **Ctrl+R**). Talk, sing, or play. In other words, send an audio signal from your input device to Vegas. As you do, you'll see the signal's audio waveform drawing into a new event in the Vegas timeline. When you're ready to stop recording, click the **Stop** button.

The **Recorded Files** dialog (shown in **Figure 3.6**) opens. If you're not happy with your performance, click the **Delete** or **Delete All** button. To rename the recorded file, click the **Rename** button and type a new name. When you're finished, click the **Done** button. A new event now holds the recorded file in the timeline, and the Media Pool contains the recorded file so that you can easily add it to the project again. Click the **Arm for Record** button in the track header to take the track out of Arm for Record mode.

Figure 3.6

Use the Recorded Files dialog to save, rename, or delete your recording.

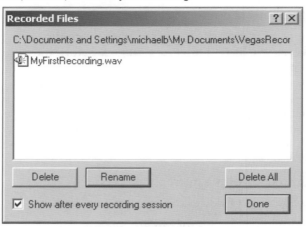

Task 7: Recording with a microphone

In this task you'll record original audio to a Vegas audio track.

1. With your microphone connected, track armed for record, and levels properly set, click the **Record** button.
2. Talk or sing into the microphone.
3. When you're done, click the **Stop** button.
4. In the Recorded Files dialog, click the **Delete** button. When asked if you are sure you want to delete the file, click **Yes**. The file no longer appears in the Recorded Files dialog.
5. Click **Done**. The track remains empty and the event that was drawn during the recording process disappears (because you deleted the file in Step 4).
6. Repeat steps 1 through 3.
7. In the Recorded Files dialog, click **Rename**, and then type "MyFirstRecording" as the new name for the recorded file.
8. Click **Done**. The new event appears in the timeline.
9. Click the **Arm for Record** button to take this track out of Arm for Record mode.

Congratulations! You've just made your first recording in Vegas!

_pt_ Private Tutor: Recording multiple tracks simultaneously

If your computer has multiple sound cards, or a sound card with multiple inputs, you can record to multiple tracks simultaneously. This is important for times when you have multiple sources of audio that you'd like to keep separated in your Vegas project. To set your project up to record two or more tracks simultaneously, choose **Windows Classic Wave Driver** from the **Audio device type** drop-down on the Audio Device tab of the Preferences dialog as shown in **Figure 3.7**. Arm each track for recording, click the track's recording device button, and choose the desired input from the shortcut menu.

Figure 3.7
Select the Windows Classic Wave Driver in the **Audio device type** drop-down.

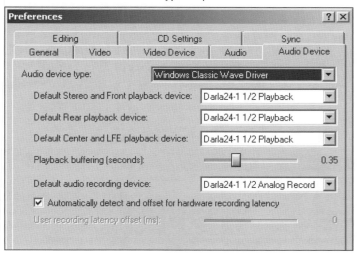

Private Tutor: Accessing the Project Recorded Files Folder dialog

pt Notice that the Project Recorded Files Folder dialog does not open the second time (or subsequent times) you arm a track for recording. It remembers the setting you chose the first time you armed a track for recording in the current project. To choose a different location for saving your recorded files, hold the **Shift** key when you click the **Arm for Record** button. This opens the Project Recorded Files Folder dialog.

Lesson 3: Extracting Audio from CD

There is yet another way to acquire audio for your project: you can extract audio from an audio CD and create a .wav file that you add to your project. You can extract individual tracks, the entire disc, or a specific range of audio on the disc.. To extract audio from an audio CD, insert the CD into your computer's CD-ROM drive (if an application automatically opens to play the CD, close it). Choose **File | Extract Audio from CD**. After Vegas runs a short search for audio devices, the Extract Audio from CD dialog opens as in **Figure 3.8**. If you have more than one CD-ROM drive in your computer, you may need to choose the drive where you inserted the CD from the **Drive** drop-down list.

Figure 3.8
The Extract Audio from CD dialog offers three ways to extract audio from a CD.

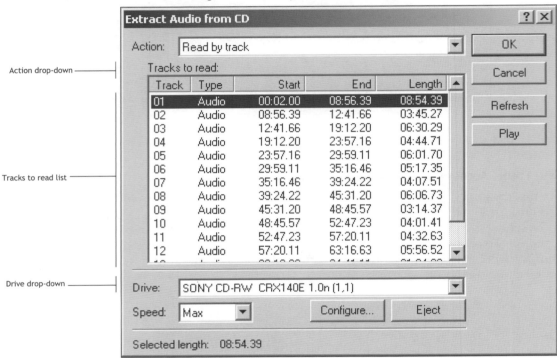

The **Action** drop-down list contains three options for extracting your music from the CD. The first choice, **Read by track**, enables you to pick the specific track or tracks to extract. Click a track in the **Tracks to read** list to select it for extraction. Use the Windows selection techniques you learned earlier to select multiple tracks for extracting. Click the **Play** button to play the selected track so you can hear the track before extracting it and make sure it's the one you want. Click **OK** to begin the extraction process. A Save As dialog opens so that you can specify a file name and a save location for the extracted file. Click **Save** when you're ready to extract the audio and create the new .wav file.

The second choice in the **Action** drop-down list, **Read entire disc**, extracts every track from the CD to one .wav file in one operation. Since you don't choose individual tracks, the **Tracks to read** list is not necessary (as shown in **Figure 3.9**) Again, when you click **OK**, the Save As dialog opens. Specify a name and save location and click **Save**. In this mode, Vegas saves all tracks to a single .wav file.

Figure 3.9
The **Read entire disc** option automatically extracts all tracks on the CD to a single .wav file.

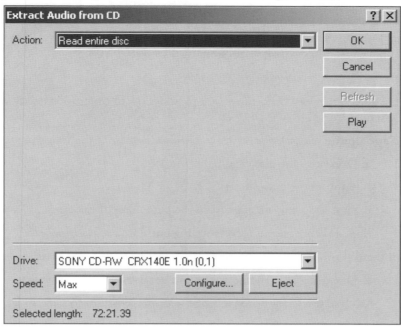

Use the third choice, **Read by range**, to select a specific start and end point to extract. This is useful in a CD where the audio you would like to extract is a portion of a long track.

Regardless of the extraction method you use, Vegas adds the extracted file (or files) to your Media Pool. This makes it very easy to add the file to your project timeline. You can also use any of the other methods you've learned for adding a file to your timeline.

Task 8: Extracting Audio from a CD

In this task you'll extract a single track from a CD.

1. Place an audio CD with at least 2 tracks in your CD ROM drive. If another application opens to play the CD, close that application.
2. In a new Vegas project choose **File | Extract Audio from CD**. Vegas may need a few moments to scan your computer for supported CD-ROM devices.
3. When the Extract Audio from CD dialog opens, choose **Read by track** from the **Action** drop-down list.
4. Click track 2 to select it.
5. Click the **Play** button to listen to the track
6. Click **OK**
6. In the Save As dialog, navigate to your My Documents folder.
7. Name the file TestExtraction in the **File name** box.
8. Click **Save**.
9. Open the Media Pool and drag the file TestExtraction.wav to the timeline.
10. Click the **Play** button and listen to the extracted audio.

Conclusion

In this module, you learned how easily you can add original media to your video projects. You learned how to set up your system for capturing video, recording audio, and extracting audio from your CD collection. You then learned how to perform these functions using the easy Vegas controls. With this knowledge, you have greatly expanded your creative horizons. In the next module, you'll learn how to add colored backgrounds and text to your projects.

Exercises

1. True or false: There are special procedures you must follow in order to install Sonic Foundry Video Capture after you've installed Vegas.

2. The **Verify Tape Name** dialog presents three options. Which of the following is not one of the options?

   a. Don't capture any clips right now

   b. Capture the current clip only

   c. Start capturing all clips from the beginning of the tape

   d. Start capturing all clips from the current tape position

3. Which two of the following options describe one aspect of how the **Shuttle** slider works?

   a. Drag the slider all the way to the left to stop video playback.

   b. Drag the slider to the left of the center position to play the video in reverse.

   c. Double-click the slider to step through the video one frame at a time.

   d. Drag the slider farther from its center position to play the video faster.

4. True or false: You should always avoid capturing heads on your video, but capturing tails is acceptable.

5. What does it mean if you end up with three captured clips even though you think you only clicked the **Capture Video** button one time?

   a. You had a momentary interruption in the communication between your DV camcorder and your capture card.

   b. You accidentally double-clicked the **Capture Video** button.

   c. Video Capture has detected three scenes on the tape during the capture procedure.

   d. You have used a low-grade DV tape, and the low quality is causing capture problems.

6. True or false: When using Sonic Foundry Video Capture, your captured clips can be added to the Media Pool automatically.

7. True or false: Once a clip is in the Media Pool, you must drag it to the Explorer Window in order to preview it and add it to the timeline.

8. Which of the following best describes a microphone-level input jack on your computer's sound card?

   a. A jack that accepts XLR plugs.

   b. An input jack that does not boost the signal coming into it.

   c. An input jack that boosts the signal coming into it.

   d. A jack that is only available on sound cards with multiple inputs.

9. True or false: You must use the **Master** fader in the Vegas Mixer to control the recording level.

10. True or false: When setting record level, you should never let the record meter peak above –6 dB.

11. Once you've recorded a file, which of the following describes how best to add it to your timeline for the first time?

        a. Vegas adds the file automatically as you record it.

        b. Double-click the file in the Media Pool.

        c. Navigate to the file in the Explorer window, and then drag it to the timeline.

        d. Right-click and drag it from the Media Pool to the timeline, and then choose **Audio Only | Add As Takes** from the shortcut menu.

12. Which of the following is not a method for extracting audio from an audio CD?

        a. Read by range.

        b. Read by track.

        c. Read entire disc.

        d. Read by song.

13. Draw a line from the keyboard shortcut to the action it performs

a. Ctrl+Shift+R	Capture Video
b. Shift+Left Arrow	Record Audio
c. Ctrl+R	Rewind (video capture)
d. Shift+Right Arrow	Capture Image
e. Ctrl+R	Fast Forward (video capture)

Essays

1. Briefly explain a situation in which you would plug your audio source into the microphone jack of your sound card. Describe a situation in which you would plug into the line-in jack. Include a discussion of why you might sometimes use a microphone as your input source, yet still plug into the line-in jack.

2. Study the Media Pool for a few minutes. Describe why the Media Pool is such a helpful feature of Vegas. Include what you learned from the brief discussion of the Media Pool contained in this module, but also explore the various buttons and come up with some ideas of your own.

3. Explain the advantages of using Sonic Foundry Video Capture in conjunction with Vegas as opposed to a third-party video capture application.

Module 4: Generating media

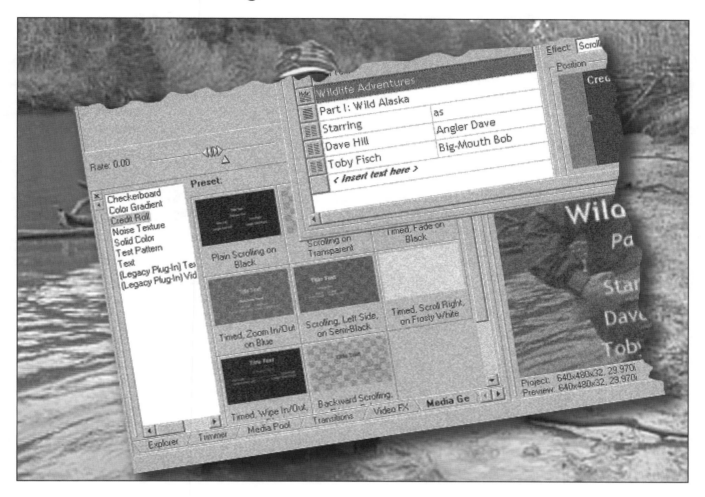

You learned in Modules 2 and 3 that there are many ways to add files to your project, but not all of the possibilities have been exhausted. All of the media you've added so far has come from outside of Vegas. You can also generate your own media inside the application. Media generators allow you to create text, test patterns, solid colors, noise textures, color gradients, and patterns that you can then use for anything from basic color backgrounds to dynamic sequences of intricate gradients with shifting colors, moving text, and more. With media generators, as you'll learn in this module, the possibilities for creative effects is unlimited. Here, you'll learn how to add media generators to your project and manipulate them to enhance your video projects.

In this module you'll learn how to do the following:

- Add backgrounds to your project.
- Create gradients that change over time.
- Add text overlays to your video.
- Quickly build interesting credit rolls.

Lesson 1: Generating solid color elements

Using Vegas media generators, you can create text and backgrounds that are completely customizable without leaving your project. In this lesson, you'll learn how to use media generators to create solid-color backgrounds and graphic design elements.

Vegas provides a few different methods you can use to add generated media to your project. First, choose **View | Plug-Ins** (**Ctrl+Alt+1**) to open the Plug-Ins window. In the Plug-Ins window, navigate to the desired media generator using the same navigation techniques that you use in the Explorer window. The tree view on the left side shows your plug-ins folder structure, and the details of the contents of the folders appear on the right side. Click the **Plus** (+) to the left of the *Video* folder. Click the folder icon for the *Media Generators* folder. The right side of the window now shows the various available media generators. Drag a generator from the Plug-Ins window to the Vegas timeline to create a new event containing the generated media. This also opens the Video Event FX window that we'll discuss a little later.

The Plug-Ins window provides a quick way to add generated media after you are familiar with what each generator does and can recognize the one you want just by looking at the name alone. However, Vegas provides a more visual method for adding generated media that you'll probably use more often.

Click the **Close** button at the top-right corner of the Video Event FX window, then do the same with the Plug-Ins window (or choose **View | Plug-Ins** to close the window). In the window docking area, click the **Media Generators** tab. This brings the Media Generators window to the front. On the left side of the Media Generators window, you see the same media generator options that you saw in the Plug-Ins window. Click any entry in the list at the left to see thumbnails (on the right) for the presets available with that particular type of media generator. Although you can use any of these presets just as they are, they are really only the tip of the iceberg; each media generator is very flexible and customizable. You'll learn more about that in a few minutes. First, let's add some media to the Vegas timeline.

The first generator in the list on the left is Checkerboard, but since the Solid Color generator is less complicated, let's start with that one. Click **Solid Color** in the list. To add one of the presets to your timeline, drag the thumbnail to the timeline.

Task 1: Adding a media generator to the timeline

In this task, you'll use the Solid Color media generator to add an event to the Vegas timeline.

1. Create a new Vegas project.
2. Click the Media Generators tab at the bottom of the window docking area. If the tab is not visible, you may need to scroll the tab area to see it or choose View | Media Generators to open it.
3. Click **Solid Color** in the list of media generators on the left side of the window.
4. Drag the *Red* preset thumbnail to the beginning of the timeline.
5. Keep this project open so you can build upon it in the next task.

Two things happen when you release the mouse button after dragging a preset thumbnail to the timeline. First, an event that holds the generated media appears on the timeline. Simultaneously, the Video Event FX window (shown in **Figure 4.1**) opens. Here you can change the parameters of the media generator from the preset that you chose in the Media Generators window.

pt Private Tutor: Resizing the Video Event FX window

It's possible that the Video Event FX window could be too small to properly display all of the parameter controls for your generated media. To make sure you're seeing all of the available controls, drag the edges of the window to resize it.

Figure 4.1
The Video Event FX window provides the controls you use to adjust the properties of your generated media.

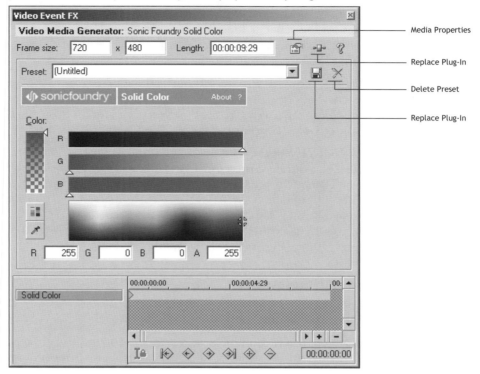

Media Properties

Replace Plug-In

Delete Preset

Replace Plug-In

Private Tutor: Changing preset parameters

You might not need to make any changes to the preset you added to your timeline. If not, go ahead and close the Video Event FX window. To avoid opening the Video Event FX window altogether, hold the **Shift** key as you drag the preset to the timeline. Often, you'll choose the preset that gets you closest to what you want and then adjust the parameters in the Video Event FX window until you create exactly what you're after.

At the top of the Video Event FX window, you can adjust the properties of the generated media. For example, the **Frame size** boxes allow you to specify the dimensions of the media. By default, the frame size for the media matches the frame size of your video project (which you set in the Project Properties dialog), but you can change it here if you want. Change the value in the **Length** box to change the duration of the generated media.

Private Tutor: Changing the length of generated media

Changing the length of the media does not change the length of the event that holds the media, so you may need to adjust the length of the event to match your new length for the media. You'll learn how to adjust the length of events in Module 6, *Basic editing techniques*, Lesson 3, *Edge trimming an event*.

The **Media Properties** button, shown in **Figure 4.1**, opens the Properties dialog where you can change many advanced properties of the media.

Private Tutor: Generated media properties

pt Although the Properties dialog gives you a great deal of control over the properties for the generated media, you'll rarely need to make any adjustments. Since the generated media takes on the properties of the project, there is usually no need to make adjustments.

The **Replace Plug-In** button (shown in **Figure 4.1**) opens the Plug-In Chooser where you can choose a different media generator than the one you originally chose. For instance, you may have originally chosen the Solid Color generator, and now decide to use the Color Gradient generator instead. In this case, click the **Replace Plug-In** button, select **Sonic Foundry Color Gradient** in the Plug-In Chooser, click **Add**, and click **OK**.

The middle section of the Video Event FX window contains the parameters of the media generator. The **Preset** drop-down list allows you to choose a different preset from the one you originally chose when you added the generated media to the project. If you change the parameters of the generator and decide that you'll want to use those settings again in the future, save the current parameter settings as a custom preset. To do so, change the parameters of the generated media (as discussed below), and select the text in the **Preset** box. Type a new preset name and click the **Save Preset** button. The preset you created now appears in the drop-down list. To remove it, select it from the list and click the **Delete Preset** button (**Figure 4.1** shows both of these buttons).

Task 2: Working with presets

The concept of presets appears in many different areas of Vegas. This task shows you how you can work with presets to streamline your editing job.

1. If the project you started in the previous task is no longer open, repeat Task 1.
2. In the Video Event FX window, choose **Blue** from the **Preset** drop-down list. The event changes from red to blue.
3. Double-click the preset name ("Blue") in the **Preset** box.
4. Type "MyNewPreset" and press **Enter**.
5. Click the **Save Preset** button.
6. Expand the **Preset** drop-down list again, and notice that **MyNewPreset** now appears in the list. Choose any preset other than **Blue** or **MyNewPreset** from the list. The event changes to the color of the preset you choose.
7. Expand the list again and choose **MyNewPreset**. The event changes again.
8. Click the **Delete Preset** button to remove the preset from the list. Keep this project open so you can use it in the next task.

The middle section of the Video Event FX window contains the controls for adjusting the media parameters. The controls for the Solid Color generator are fairly simple and give you a number of ways to change the color of the generated media. The four sliders (one vertical and three horizontal) provide a visual method of choosing the color you want. Drag the small triangle below the **R** (red) color bar to adjust the amount of red you want to include in the color. Do the same to adjust the amount of green (the **G** color bar) and blue (the **B** color bar). Use the vertical slider to adjust the alpha channel of the generated media.

Private Tutor: Changing the alpha channel value

pt The alpha channel controls transparency. The maximum alpha value (255) creates completely opaque media. The minimum value (0) creates completely transparent media. If you choose an alpha value of 0, it doesn't really matter what color you make your media because no one can see it anyway! The checkerboard background in the alpha channel control indicates transparency. The more clearly you can see the checkerboard pattern, the more transparent the color (that is, the lower the alpha value). As you adjust the alpha value, the event in the timeline also reflects the amount of transparency (again, as represented by the checkerboard pattern in the event itself). Transparency allows you to see through the event on the top track of your project to an event on a track below it. This is one form of compositing, a topic we discuss in Module 7, *Enhancing your project*, Lesson 6, *Video composites*.

Below the color bars, you find a color picker. This area enables you to quickly select the color you want. To choose a color, click anywhere within the color picker. Note that you cannot control the alpha value with the color picker. To choose white as your color, drag to the top of the picker area. To choose black, drag to the bottom. When you drag to the top or bottom (or any other time all three color values are exactly equal), a slider appears on the right edge of the picker. This slider allows you to quickly choose a level of gray as your color.

Four color boxes appear below the color picker. (If the Video Event FX window may be too small to show these boxes, drag the edges of the Video Event window to make it larger.) These fields allow you to enter an exact value for the red (**R**), green (**G**), blue (**B**), and alpha (**A**) channels of the color. This is handy if you already know the exact values for the color you want.

The **Pick Color from Screen** button, shown in **Figure 4.2**, allows you to choose a color from anywhere on your computer screen. Click the **Pick Color from Screen** button and then click the color you want. The object you click need not be part of Vegas.

Figure 4.2

The Pick Color from Screen enables you to choose a color from anywhere on your computer screen.

Above the **Pick Color from Screen** button is a toggle switch that allows you to change the color model you are using from the RGB (red-green-blue) model (described here) to the HSL (hue-saturation-luminance) model. Both models are simply different ways to choose and work with colors, and you can use whichever one is easiest for you.

Task 3: Changing the color parameters

In this task, you'll use several different techniques to choose the color for your media generator.

1. If the project you worked on in the previous task is no longer open, use the Solid Color media generator to add an event at the beginning of the timeline in a new project. Choose the **Red** preset.
2. In the Video Event FX window, drag the green color slider (G) all the way to the right. This changes the color of the event to yellow.
3. Drag in the color picker to see how the color changes. Release the mouse button somewhere in the green portion of the chooser to set the color to a shade of green.
4. In the color boxes below the color picker, enter 100 in the R box, 20 in the G box, and 133 in the B box. This creates a purple color.
5. Click the **Pick Color from Screen** button.
6. Click the yellow part of the Vegas logo in the Vegas title bar (at the top-left corner of the Vegas window). This samples the color and sets the event to that color.
7. Click the **Pick Color from Screen** button again and click anywhere else on your computer screen to sample the color there.

You will become very familiar with the bottom section of the Video Event FX window, not so much because you'll use if often with generated media (although you might), but because you'll see it in many windows in Vegas. This area—the keyframe controller—enables you to change the parameters you set for your generated media over time within the same media event and control the way Vegas transitions between the different parameter settings. Because it is so important to understand the concepts behind the keyframe controller, we'll spend the next lesson exploring how it works.

For now, once you've adjusted the parameters in the Video Event FX window, click the **Close** button in the upper-right corner of the window to close the window. If you later decide to change the parameters of the generated media, click the **Generated Media** button on the event that holds the generated media (see **Figure 4.3**). Alternatively, right-click the event and choose **Edit Generated Media** from the shortcut menu. Either of these methods opens the Video Event FX window.

Figure 4.3
Click the **Generated Media** button in the event to open the Video Event FX window and adjust the parameters.

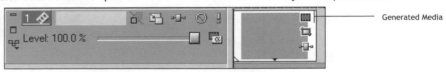

Generated Media

Lesson 2: Using the keyframe controller

In this lesson, you'll learn techniques that you'll use many times while working with Vegas. The keyframe controller appears at the bottom of various windows throughout the application. **Figure 4.4** shows the keyframe controller in the Video Event FX window. Mastering keyframe techniques opens up a huge array of possibilities.

Figure 4.4
The keyframe controller gives you countless ways to customize your project.

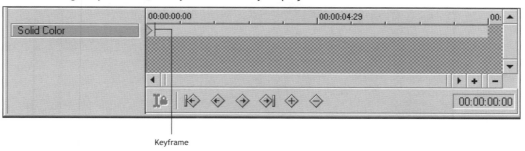

Keyframe

Click the **Generated Media** button on an event that holds generated media to open the Video Event FX window. At the moment, there's not much going on in the keyframe controller, but let's take a look at what's there. On the left, a label identifies this as the keyframe controller for an event that holds media created with the Solid Color generator. Since it is the only keyframe bar showing, it is automatically selected and ready for you to edit.

The keyframe timeline appears to the right of the label. At the top, the time ruler indicates the length of the generated media. Just below the time ruler, the keyframe timeline holds the keyframes associated with the generated media. There must always be at least one keyframe, and by default one keyframe appears at the beginning of the timeline as shown in **Figure 4.4**. When only one keyframe exists in the timeline, it defines the parameters of the generated media for its entire duration, regardless of where on the timeline it appears.

Private Tutor: What is a keyframe?

For purposes of this discussion, a keyframe defines the state of an object (in this case, the parameters of the generated media) at a specific point in time.

The timeline can hold as many keyframes as you want to add. Therefore, you can create additional keyframes in the timeline and change the parameters of the generated media at those new keyframes. Thus, you can create a generated media event with parameter settings that change over time. In other words, you can add keyframes to create a generated media event that starts out as one color, but ends up a different color by the time it reaches the end.

Across the bottom of the keyframe controller are several buttons (see **Figure 4.5**). The first button, the **Sync Cursor** button, cannot be used with generated media, so we'll defer discussion of that button until Module 7, *Enhancing your project*, Lesson 6, *Video composites*. We'll also skip over the next four buttons for just a moment, and talk first about the **Create Keyframe** button.

To create a new keyframe, click the keyframe timeline at the point where you want the keyframe to appear. Alternatively, double-click the value in the timeline's **Cursor Position** box, type a new value, and press the **Tab** key. The orange, flashing cursor moves to the point you chose. Click the **Create Keyframe** button to add a new keyframe at the cursor position. In **Figure 4.5**, you can see that the new keyframe looks different from the first keyframe in two ways. First, it is a full diamond, and second, it contains a small white diamond. The different shape is merely a result of the first keyframe being at the very beginning of the timeline, and the white inner diamond identifies the currently selected keyframe.

Figure 4.5

Add as many keyframes as you need to the keyframe controller.

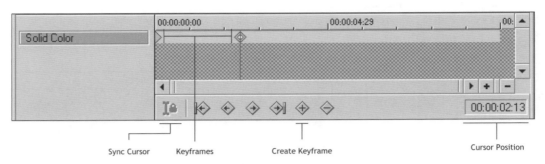

When you change the parameters of the media generator, the changes apply to only the currently selected keyframe.

Task 4: Creating additional keyframes

This task shows you how to create additional keyframes for an event holding generated media.

1. Add a solid color media generator to a new project. Use the **Blue** preset.
2. Click the middle of the keyframe timeline to position the cursor.
3. Click the **Create Keyframe** button to add a keyframe.
4. Double-click the **Cursor Position** field for the keyframe timeline to select the current value.
5. Type "8.15" and press the **Tab** key to place the cursor at 8 second, 15 frames.
6. Click the **Create Keyframe** button again to add another keyframe. You now have three keyframes. Keep this project open so you can use it in the next task.

Let's return to the four buttons we skipped earlier. You can use these buttons, shown in **Figure 4.6**, to navigate quickly from one keyframe to another. The **First Keyframe** button takes you to the first keyframe in the timeline. The **Previous Keyframe** button takes you to the keyframe to the left of the currently selected keyframe. The **Next Keyframe** button takes you to the keyframe to the right of the currently selected keyframe. The **Last Keyframe** button takes you to the last keyframe in the timeline. You can also click the desired keyframe to select it.

Figure 4.6

The buttons in the keyframe controller.

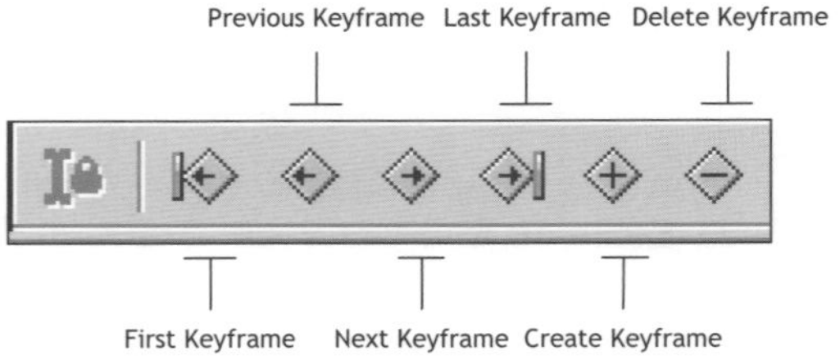

Previous Keyframe Last Keyframe Delete Keyframe

First Keyframe   Next Keyframe Create Keyframe

pt **Private Tutor: Selecting multiple keyframes**

Once again, those standard Windows selection techniques (using the Shift key and Ctrl key) come in handy because they allow you to select multiple keyframes simultaneously.

To remove a keyframe, select it and then click the **Delete Keyframe** button. Alternatively, select the keyframe and press the **Delete** key on your computer keyboard. You can also cut, copy, and paste keyframes. To do so, right-click a keyframe and choose the desired command from the shortcut menu. To reposition a keyframe, drag it to a new spot on the timeline.

Task 5: Selecting and manipulating keyframes

In this task, you'll use the techniques you just learned to navigate to and manipulate the keyframes you added in the previous task.

1. If the project you started in the previous task is no longer open, repeat the previous task.
2. Click the **First Keyframe** button to select the first keyframe.
3. Click the **Next Keyframe** button to select the next keyframe in the timeline.
4. Type "9.0" into the **Cursor Position** box and press **Enter**.
5. Drag the last keyframe in the timeline to the right until it snaps to the cursor at 9.0 seconds.
6. Right-click the middle keyframe and choose **Copy** from the shortcut menu.
7. Click between the first and second keyframes to reposition the cursor.
8. Right-click the timeline (but not on a keyframe) and choose **Paste** from the shortcut menu to paste a keyframe at the cursor position.
9. Click the third keyframe in the timeline and press the **Delete** key to remove the keyframe.

You can also define how you want Vegas to handle the transition from one keyframe to the next. By default, the first keyframe transitions into the next evenly along a linear transition path. To change the transition style, right-click the first keyframe and choose a command from the shortcut menu:

- **Hold**—The parameters of the first keyframe remain active until the cursor reaches the second keyframe, at which point the parameters of the second keyframe take over immediately. No transition exists between the two keyframes.
- **Linear**—The parameters of the first keyframe transition evenly into the parameters of the second keyframe.
- **Fast**—The transition starts out fast, and then slows down as it approaches the second keyframe.
- **Slow**—The opposite of the Fast transition style described above. The transition starts out slowly, and then picks up speed as it reaches the second keyframe.
- **Smooth**—Here, the transition starts out slowly, speeds up until reaching the midpoint between the two keyframes, and then slows down again as it approaches the second keyframe.

> *pt* **Private Tutor: Quickly identifying the transition style**
>
> Vegas supplies color cues so you can quickly see what transition style has been applied to your keyframes. Red indicates a keyframe set to "Hold," gray indicates "Linear," green means "Fast," yellow means "Slow," and blue indicates that the transition is set to "Smooth."

Task 6: Keyframes—putting it all together

You now know how to use the keyframe controller. In this task, you'll use what you know to create generated media that transitions from one color to another.

1. In a new Vegas project, add a solid color generated media event to the very beginning of a new project. Use the **Blue** preset.
2. Click the end of the keyframe timeline to place the cursor, and then click the **Create Keyframe** button to add a new keyframe at the end of the timeline.
3. With the new keyframe still selected, move the slider for the red (**R**) component of the color all the way to the right and the slider for the blue (**B**) component all the way to the left.
4. Click the **Play** button to play your project. Watch as the Video Preview window transitions evenly from blue to red according to the linear transition style between the two keyframes.
5. Right-click the first keyframe and choose **Slow** from the shortcut menu.

6. Play the project again, and notice that this time the transition from blue to red starts out slowly and picks up speed as it approaches the second keyframe.
7. Add a new keyframe between the two existing keyframes. Use the color boxes to set the color parameters to **R**=0, **G**=255, and **B**=0.
8. Right-click the middle keyframe and notice in the shortcut menu that the transition style matches that of the keyframe directly before it. Choose **Smooth** from the shortcut menu.
9. Right-click the first keyframe and choose **Hold** from the shortcut menu.
10. Play the project and watch as the event remains blue until it reaches the second keyframe, at which point it turns instantly to green, and then transitions to red as it reaches the end keyframe. Notice that the transition style of the last keyframe has no effect because there is no keyframe into which to transition.

pt **Private Tutor: Using a shortcut to create keyframes**

You can quickly create a new keyframe without clicking the **Create Keyframe** button. To do so, click the keyframe timeline to reposition the cursor. Now, go directly to the parameters section and change any attribute of the media generator. As soon as you make an adjustment, Vegas adds a new keyframe to the timeline.

In the next few lessons, we'll resume our discussion of other types of media generators.

Lesson 3: Generating color gradients

Now that you know how media generators work, you can use any of the available generators in Vegas. The main differences between the various generators are the contents of the media each one creates, and (based on that) what parameters can be changed within the generator. In this lesson, you'll explore a generator that is closely related to the Solid Color generator you studied in the previous lesson: the Color Gradient generator.

The Color Gradient generator offers many more possibilities than Solid Color generator. Click **Color Gradient** in the list of media generators in the Media Generators window. Take a moment to look at all of the gradient options. Several of the presets contain the checkerboard pattern that indicates transparency, and these can be used to create special effects. Others have no transparency, and these would typically be used as backgrounds or graphic design elements, much like the Solid Color generator. Add a Color Gradient generator to your project just as you've added the other generators.

The Video Event FX window contains more parameters for the Color Gradient generator than for the Solid Color generator we studied earlier. Let's start with what you already know. Below the **Distance** box in the **Control Point Properties** section you'll recognize the same color controls used with the Solid Color media generator.

To create gradients (sometimes called blends), the Color Gradient generator assigns color attributes to two or more control points. It then creates a gradient between each point and the next-closest point (or points) to it. To see how this works, choose the *Linear Red, Green and Blue* preset in the Video Event FX window. This gradient contains three control points, as you can see in the **Control Points** section of the Video Event FX window. Click control point #1 to display its color properties in the **Control Point Properties** section. You can change the point's properties if you want using the techniques you learned earlier.

Click control point #2 to display or change its color properties. Notice that control point #1 is set to blue, and point #2 is set to green. Vegas builds a blue-to-green blend between the two points. A similar blend goes from the green of point #2 to the red of point #3.

Task 7: Changing the colors of control points

This task shows you how to change the color of control points to create a custom blend based on a preset.

1. In a new project, click **Color Gradient** in the list of media generators on the left side of the Media Generators window.
2. Drag the **Linear White to Black** preset to the timeline to create a new gradient.
3. Two control points create this gradient. Click control point #1 (at the far left of the Control Points area) to display the properties for that point.
4. Set the color for control point #1 to **R**=255, **G**=0, **B**=0. The control point changes to red, and the gradient now goes from red to black instead of white to black.
5. Click control point #2 (at the far right of the area). Change its color to **R**=0, **G**=255, **B**=0. The gradient now blends from red at point #1 to green at point #2.

You can also drag control points within the Control Points area to further modify a gradient. As you move points closer together, the gradient between them becomes less gradual. When you change a point's position along an imaginary line that runs through all of the points, the value in the **Distance** box of the Control Point Properties section updates accordingly. This value reflects the point's distance from the center of the Control Points field (identified by the white cross). You can type a new value in the box if you know exactly where you want to position the point.

When you change the position of a control point in any direction other than exactly along an imaginary line that runs through all of the points, you also affect every other control point and change the blend angle. This causes the value in the **Aspect Ratio Angle** box to change. If you know an exact angle you want to use for the blend, enter it in the **Aspect Ratio Angle** box.

Private Tutor: Moving a point off axis

pt

All points are always in a straight line. In other words, they must always share the same axis. Therefore, if you move one point off of the line, all the other points have to move in order to maintain the line through them. The axis remains perpendicular to the blend angle in a linear blend. In elliptical and rectangular blends (which we'll discuss in a few minutes), the blend angle affects the shape of the blend.

You can also move the center of the control points to a new location by dragging them to the desired location. When you click the center cross, the **X** and **Y** boxes replace the **Distance** box in the Control Point Properties section. You can type values in the **X** and **Y** boxes to specify an exact location for the center point.

Task 8: Repositioning control points

This task shows you how reposition control points and the center point to modify your gradient.

1. From the **Preset** drop-down list in the Video Event FX window, choose **Linear Red, Green and Blue**.
2. Double-click the **Aspect Ratio Angle** box to highlight the current value, type "0.0," and press **Enter** to change the blend angle.
3. Drag control point **#1** to the top, center of the Control Points area. The other points move as necessary to maintain the axis through the three control points, and the blend angle changes accordingly.
4. Move control point **#3** up toward point **#2**. The blend between the two points becomes more sudden as the two points converge.

So far, we've worked only with linear gradients, but Vegas offers two other options: elliptical and rectangular. Choose a preset to add one of these types of gradient or choose the type you want from the **Gradient Type** drop-down list.

Task 9: Creating different gradient types

In this task, you'll learn how to work with elliptical and rectangular gradients.

1. From the **Preset** drop-down list in the Video Event FX window, choose **Elliptical White to Black**.
2. Experiment with the two control points and the center position to get an idea of how you can customize the gradient.
3. After experimenting, choose **Elliptical White to Black** from the **Preset** drop-down list again to restore the gradient.
4. Notice that there is no **Rectangular White to Black** preset, but you can easily create one. From the **Gradient Type** drop-down list, choose **Rectangular**.
5. Double-click the **Preset** box to select the current value, and type "Rectangular White to Black."
6. Click the **Save Preset** button. You now have a **Rectangular White to Black** preset.

Private Tutor: Grabbing a hidden center point

pt

In Task 10, *Creating different gradient types* you added the **Elliptical White to Black** preset to your project. Earlier you learned that you can change the center point of the Control Points area. But you might notice that if you want to change the center point of the **Elliptical White to Black** preset, you have a problem: control point #1 prevents you from grabbing the center point. To get around this problem, right-click the Control Points area and choose **Reset**. This selects the center point, and you can now drag it to a new position. Experiment with different center points for elliptical and rectangular gradients; you'll find that you can create many interesting effects.

To further modify a gradient, you can add or delete control points. The bottom of the Control Point area displays four buttons you can use to work with control points. Click the **Add a new gradient control point** button to place a new control point into your gradient. You can then change the position and attributes of the new control point to achieve the desired gradient effect. Click the **Remove currently selected gradient control point** button to delete the currently selected control point. Click the **Select previous gradient control point** button to select the control point with the next lowest number from the currently selected point. Click the **Select next gradient control point** button to select the control point with the next highest number.

Task 10: Working with control points

This task shows you how to use the control point buttons to select control points, and add and delete control points. You'll learn how additional control points help create many different blend effects.

1. From the **Preset** drop-down list of the Video Event FX window, choose **Linear White to Black**.
2. Click the **Add a new gradient control point** button to add a new control point.
3. Move the new point so that it sits over the center point.
4. Adjust the color parameters of the new point to **R**=255, **G**=0, **B**=0, **A**=255. The colors now blend from white to red, and then from red to black.
5. Click the **Select previous gradient control point** button to select control point #2.
6. Change the colors of point #2 to **R**=0, **G**=0, **B**=255. The colors now blend from white to red, and then from red to blue.

The final two buttons change the number assigned to the selected control point. The **Increase gradient control point position number** button swaps the number assigned to the selected control point with the control point that contains the next highest number. For example, with control point #2 selected, this button causes button #2 to be labeled "3" and button #3 to be labeled "2." The **Decrease gradient control point position number** button has the opposite effect.

In many cases, the button order makes no difference, but the button order does come into play when you use the keyframe controller to create transitions from the settings at one keyframe to different settings at the next. In this case, Vegas blends control point #1 at the first keyframe to control point #1 at the second keyframe. Point #2 blends to the #2 at the new keyframe, #3 to # 3, and so on. To create interesting effects, change the order of the buttons at the second keyframe and experiment to see what happens during the transition from the first keyframe to the next.

Task 11: Reordering control points to create interesting effects

In this task, you'll manipulate control points to create different transitional effects between two keyframes.

1. From the **Preset** drop-down list in the Video Event FX window, choose **Linear Red, Green and Blue**.
2. Click near the midpoint of the keyframe timeline to place the cursor.
3. Type "-45.0" in the **Aspect Ratio Angle** box and press the **Tab** key. This creates a new keyframe.
4. Play your project and notice how the keyframes cause the blend to change as Vegas transitions from the first keyframe to the next.
5. Click the end of the keyframe timeline and type "-90.0" in the **Aspect Ratio Angle** box. Again, this creates a new keyframe.
6. Play your project to see how it looks to this point.
7. Click the last keyframe to select it.
8. Click control point #1 to select it, and then click the **Increase gradient control point position number** button twice. What was control point #1 is now #3.
9. Click control point #1 (which is now the middle control point), and then click the **Increase gradient control point position number** button once. The control points now start with #1 at the top of the Control Points area, #2 in the middle, and #3 at the bottom.
10. Play your project, and notice how changing the order of the points has changed the effect you achieve.

Private Tutor: Exploring endless possibilities

pt

Imagine how you can add or delete control points, change the color attributes of control points, and even change the gradient type from one keyframe to another to create even more interesting effects. Now you're learning how the keyframe controller makes Vegas truly limitless in terms of customizing effects.

Lesson 4: Generating basic text elements

Vegas also provides four media generators to add text to your movies. Two of these generators, labeled "Legacy Plug-In," are included to support the text you built in earlier versions of Vegas or Sonic Foundry's other video-editing program, Video Factory™. We won't spend time talking about these since you'll use them only for old projects. Of the remaining text generators in Vegas, the Text generator is the most basic, so let's talk about it first. In this lesson, you'll learn how to create great-looking text for your videos.

To add the Text media generator, click **Text** in the list at the left side of the Media Generators window. Look at the various preset thumbnails to see what's available. Some of the presets have solid backgrounds, while most have transparent backgrounds. You can use transparent backgrounds to create text overlays where you see the text printed over another clip in your movie. Some of the text in the examples is very simple, while some of the text has been treated with special effects.

To add text to your project, drag a preset to the timeline. The parameters area in the Video Event FX window for the Text generator contains four tabs (shown in **Figure 4.7**). On the **Edit** tab, you see controls that you probably recognize from using other Windows applications that support text. The **Font** drop-down list sets the typeface you want to use for your text. Specify how large you want your text to be in the **Size** box, or choose a size from the **Size** drop-down list. The **Bold** and **Italic** buttons apply those attributes to your text. The three alignment buttons allow you to specify left, center, or right alignment. In the lower portion of the **Edit** tab, the words "Sample Text" appear as a placeholder. Select the sample text and then type your text.

Figure 4.7
Control the look of your text in the Edit tab of the Video Event FX Window.

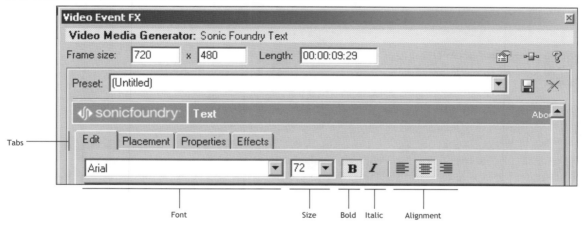

Tabs

Font   Size   Bold Italic   Alignment

Task 12: Adding a text event to the timeline

This task takes you through the process of adding text media. Here you'll learn how to adjust type font, size, and other attributes.

1. In the Media Generators window, click **Text** in the list of media generators on the left side.
2. Drag the **Solid Background** preset thumbnail to the timeline. This adds the text event and opens the Video Event FX window.
3. From the **Font** drop-down list, choose **Comic Sans MS**. (If you don't have this font on your computer, any other font will do for this task.)
4. From the **Size** drop-down list, choose **24**.
5. The **Bold** button is selected by default, and the **Italic** button is not. Click each of these buttons to see how they affect the text. Click them again to reset the text to the default state.
6. Click the **Align Left** and **Align Right** buttons to see how they affect the text. Click the **Align Center** button to restore center alignment.

7. Select the words "Sample Text" and type "My First Text." Press the Enter key after the first and second words so that each word sits on a separate line.
8. Keep this project open so you can use it in the next task.

Once you've made all your choices on the **Edit** tab, click the **Placement** tab. On the left side of the **Placement** tab parameters area, the **Text Placement** area allows you to specify exactly where you want the text to appear on the screen. Choose a preset position, type exact location coordinates into the **X** and **Y** boxes, or drag the sample text in the box to any location you desire.

Notice the red box within the Text Placement area. This box represents the safe zone. The safe zone indicates the area within which you can safely position your text. Because television screens overscan (cut off part of) the picture, objects you position toward the edge of your computer screen may be cut off on a TV screen. The safe zone helps you keep your text within an area that remains visible on most televisions. In the **Safe Zone** box, you can change the size of your safe zone.

Task 13: Adjusting text placement

In this task you'll learn how to position your text so that it appears exactly where you want it on the screen.

1. If the project you started in the previous task is no longer open, repeat Task 13, *Adding a text event to the timeline.*
2. Click the **Placement** tab.
3. Choose **Bottom Right** from the **Preset** drop-down list to position the text there.
4. Drag the text toward the top-left corner.
5. Leave this project open so you can continue with it in the next task.

Private Tutor: Using the safe zone

pt If your video will never be shown on a TV monitor, then you may not need to worry about the safe zone at all. Still, it's a good idea to keep your text away from the edges of the video even if the video will only be viewed on another computer. Notice that certain presets use the edge of the safe zone for positioning.

To edit the your text properties, click the **Properties** tab. In the **Text Color** section, you see color controls that allow you to specify the color of the text. In the **Background Color** section, you can manipulate the color of the background on which the text appears.

Private Tutor: Adjusting the size of the Video Event FX window

pt If the Video Event FX window cuts off some of the controls near the right edge of the window, you'll need to resize the window. Like any window in Vegas, hover over the edge of the window. When the cursor changes to the Resize cursor, drag the window edge until you can see all of the controls in the window.

The **Text Properties** section at the bottom of the **Properties** tab contains controls you haven't seen yet in Vegas, although you may be familiar with them if you use word processing or desktop publishing applications. The **Tracking** slider controls the amount of space between letters in your text. The **Scaling** slider allows you to make fine size adjustments to the text. With the **Leading** (which rhymes with bedding) slider, you control the amount of space between lines of text.

At larger font sizes, the space between some pairs of letters can look awkward or unnatural, while other combinations of letters look fine. In such a case, you don't want to adjust the space between all letters (with the **Tracking** slider). Instead, you need to control the space between problem letter pairs (a process known as kerning). For instance, perhaps the space between a small "i" and a small "v" looks wrong at larger sizes. To fix the problem, select the **Kern**

fonts at check box, and specify the text size at which you want kerning to activate in the **Pts and above** box. Vegas uses an internal set of kerning instructions to fix potential problems.

Task 14: Manipulating text properties

This task shows how to use the controls on the **Properties** tab of the Video Event FX window to change the appearance of your text.

1. If the project you worked on in the previous task is no longer open, repeat Task 14, *Adjusting text placement*.
2. Click the **Properties** tab in the Video Event FX window.
3. Using the **Text Color** controls, set the text color to **R**=120, **G**=255, **B**=219.
4. Using the **Background Color** controls, set the background color to **R**=200, **G**=0, **B**=100. Leave the **Alpha** value set to 255, but realize that to create text overlays, you can decrease the **Alpha** value to create transparency.
5. Drag the **Tracking** slider all the way to the right, and then the left to see how far you can spread and squeeze the text. Double-click the **Tracking** slider to return it to its default position.
6. Drag the **Scaling** slider all the way to the right, then to the left, and notice how large and small you can make the text using this control. Double-click the **Scaling** slider to return it to its default position.
7. Drag the **Leading** slider all the way to the right, and then to the left to see the range of space between lines. Double-click the **Leading** slider to return it to its default position.
8. Click the **Edit** tab, and choose **Arial** from the **Font** drop-down list. Change the font size to 72. You may need to click the **Placement** tab and reposition the text. Click the **Properties** tab to further adjust the properties.
9. In the Video Preview window, look at the "T" and the "e" in the word "Text." The space between them is large enough that they almost look as if they are not in the same word. While keeping your eye on the word "Text," select the **Kern fonts at** check box to activate kerning. Notice that Vegas decreases the space between the two letters to make them look like a more natural pair.
10. Keep this project open so you can continue with it in the next task.

pt Private Tutor: Tricks with sliders

In the Task 15, *Manipulating text properties*, you double-clicked various sliders to set them to their default values. This trick works the same throughout Vegas. Any time you want to reset a slider to its default value, double-click it. Another technique that helps when working with sliders allows you to make fine adjustments. You might notice that it can be difficult to hit an exact value with a slider because small slider movements cause large jumps in the slider value. To overcome this problem, hold the **Ctrl** key while you drag a slider. Alternatively, hold down the left and right mouse buttons simultaneously while you drag the slider. Either method forces the slider to move in much smaller increments.

The **Effects** tab allows you to add outlines and shadows, as well as adjustable deformation effects. Select the **Draw Outline** check box to add an outline to your text. Click the color square to choose the color of the outline. Use the **Feather** slider to adjust how gradually the outline fades into the background and the **Width** slider to adjust the width of the outline.

Select the **Draw Shadow** check box to put a shadow under the text (known as a drop shadow). Click the color square to choose the color for the shadow. As with the outline feature, the **Feather** control adjusts how gradually the shadow fades into the background. Use the **X Offset** slider to move the shadow away from the original text horizontally, and the **Y Offset** to move the shadow vertically.

Task 15: Manipulating text properties

This task shows how to use the controls on the **Properties** tab of the Video Event FX window to change the appearance of your text.

1. If the project you worked on in the previous task is no longer open, repeat Task 15, *Manipulating text properties*.
2. Click the **Effects** tab.
3. Select the **Draw Outline** check box to turn on the outline.
4. Click the color square, and set the outline color to **R**=255, **G**= 151, **B**=102.
5. Drag the **Feather** slider to 0.5.
6. Drag the **Width** slider to 1.0. These settings create a glowing effect.
7. Select the **Draw Outline** check box again to turn the outline off.
8. Select the **Draw Shadow** check box to turn on the shadow.
9. Double-click the **X Offset** box and type ".250." Set the **Y Offset** box to .250 also.
10. Leave this project open so you can continue working on it in the next task.

To add special deformation effects to your text, select the **Enable Deformation** check box. Choose from among the options in the **Type** drop-down list. Adjust the amount of the deformation using the **Amount** slider.

Task 16: Adding deformations to text

This task shows how to use the controls on the **Properties** tab of the Video Event FX window to change the appearance of your text.

1. If the project you worked on in the previous task is no longer open, repeat Task 16, *Manipulating text properties*.
2. From the **Type** drop-down list, choose **Bend Horizontally**.
3. Drag the **Amount** slider all the way left, and then all the way right to see just how much you can bend the text.
4. Try the other options in the **Type** drop-down list to get a feel for the different deformations you can create.

pt Private Tutor: Don't forget to set up keyframes

You can set up all kinds of special effects on your text with the keyframe controller. For instance, you could add a series of keyframes that turn the text from straight to deformed, and from red to blue to black to green. Once again, the possibilities are absolutely endless, and only the limits of your creativity (and good taste) stand in the way of interesting text effects.

Lesson 5: Generating scrolling text elements

You could easily use the keyframe controller along with the **Text** media generator that you studied in Lesson 4, *Generating basic text elements*, to create moving text like you see at the end of your favorite Hollywood blockbuster (known as scrolling text or a credit roll). However, the Credit Roll media generator makes the job even easier. In this lesson, you'll learn how to use the Credit Roll media generator.

To add scrolling text to your project, click **Credit Roll** in the list of media generators in the Media Generators window. Take a moment to hover over the various preset thumbnails. Since these presets all have motion built into them, the thumbnails are animated to show you the motion you will get when you choose the thumbnail. Drag the desired thumbnail to the timeline.

You can use three line types in the Credit Roll generator: header, single item, and dual item. In the **Credits Text** section of the Video Event FX window, you can add as many of each type as you want. By default, each preset has four lines of text: one heading, followed by one single-column entry, followed by two two-column entries. To create additional lines, click the blank square next to where it says, "<Insert text here>" and choose the appropriate icon from the menu. To delete a line, click the icon for the line and press the **Delete** key. To change an existing line from one line type to another, click the icon for the line type and choose the icon for the desired line type from the menu.

To change the content of a line, double-click the text area for that line and type the new content.

Task 17: Creating scrolling text

In this task, you'll create your first credit roll using the Credit Roll generator.

1. Click **Credit Roll** in the list of media generators in the Media Generators window.
2. Drag the **Plain Scrolling on Black** preset thumbnail to the timeline. This adds the event to the timeline and opens the Video Event FX window.
3. Double-click the content area of the first line to select the words "Title Text."
4. Type "My First Credit Roll."
5. In the same way, type "A movie by me" in the second line. Then type "Starring" in the left column of the next line and "As" in the right column of the same line. In the fourth line, type "Dash Riprock" on the left and "Slip Skidmoore" on the right.
6. Click the blank square at the beginning of the last line and choose the icon for a Dual Item (shown in **Figure 4.8**) from the menu. In the left column, type "Heather Heavenly" and in the right field, "Destiny S. Curves."

Figure 4.8
Choose Dual Item for a new row in the Credits Text section.

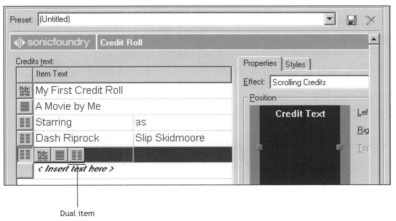

Dual item

7. Play the movie, and watch the Video Preview window to view your first credit roll.
8. Keep this project open. You'll build upon it in the next task.

The **Properties** tab contains controls that enable you to define the behavior of the text on the screen. From the **Effect** drop-down list, choose **Scrolling Credits** to make the kind of credit roll you created in Task 18, *Creating scrolling text*. Choose **Timed Sequence** to create other effects for the entry of text onto the screen and its exit from the screen.

The **Position** section determines where to place the text on the screen. Specify the left and right positions, and (for a timed sequence) the distance the text should appear from the top of the screen.

For scrolling credits, choose the scroll direction from the **Scroll Direction** drop-down list in the **Effect Parameters** section. For a timed sequence, use this section to specify the effects with which the text should enter and exit the screen. Also, specify how much text should appear at one time in the **Display** drop-down list.

Task 18: Setting credit roll properties

This task shows you how to use the controls in the **Properties** tab to control credit roll behavior.

1. If the project you started in the previous task is no longer open, repeat Task 18, *Creating scrolling text*.
2. With **Scrolling Credits** selected in the **Effect** drop-down list, drag the gold position handles to define the right and left position of the text. When you're done experimenting, right-click the position box and choose **Reset** from the shortcut menu to restore the default settings.
3. Choose **Down (Backward)** from the **Scroll Direction** drop-down list.
4. Play the project and watch as your credits roll by in the opposite direction.
5. Choose **Up (Forward)** from the **Scroll Direction** drop-down list.
6. Choose **Timed Sequence** from the **Effect** drop-down list.
7. Choose **Fast Fade In** from the **In** drop-down list.
8. Choose **Zoom Out** from the **Out** drop-down list.
9. Choose **One at a Time** from the **Display** drop-down list.
10. Play your project, and watch your new credit roll.
11. Keep this project open so that you can build on it in the next task.

The **Styles** tab contains controls that let you define the appearance of the text in your credit rolls. To define the style for each type of credit line, choose the name of the line from the **Name** drop-down list and then make adjustments to the controls. Most of the controls are familiar to you from working with basic text back in Lesson 4, *Generating basic text elements*. The two unique controls—**Space Above** and **Space Below**—enable you to set the amount of space between one line and the next.

When you choose **Dual Item** from the **Name** drop-down list, several new options appear. Font-related selections now exist for each text column so they can be set independently. The **Center Width** slider adjusts the amount of space between the left and right entries when you use the "Align Center" style, and the **Connect Sides With** drop-down list provides several options for creating a visual connection between the two columns. Set the background color with the **Background Color** box at the bottom of the **Styles** tab. The controls and options on the **Styles** tab are the same whether your credit roll is a timed sequence or rolling credit as described above.

Task 19: Defining the text line styles

In this task, you'll modify the appearance of each of the text line styles.

1. If the project you worked on in the previous task is no longer open, repeat Task 19, *Setting credit roll properties*.
2. Choose **Scrolling Credits** from the **Effect** drop-down list.
3. Click the **Styles** tab.
4. Choose **Header** from the **Name** drop-down list.
5. Choose **Impact** as the font, set the font size to 36, and click the font color square to set the font color to **R**=255, **G**=150, **B**=0.

6. To add extra space after the main headline, adjust the **Space Below** slider to .25 (slide it all the way to the right).
7. Choose **Single Item** from the **Name** drop-down list.
8. Set the font to **Comic Sans MS**, the font size to 28, and click the font color square to set the font color to **R**=255, **G**=0, **B**=0.
9. Set the **Space Below** slider to 1.000.
10. Choose **Dual Item** from the **Name** drop-down list. Notice that there are several new options. For instance, font-related selections now exist for each text column so they can be set independently.
11. Move the **Center Width** slider to .125. This adjusts the distance between the two columns.
12. Choose **Dashes** from the **Connect Sides With** drop-down list to add a dashed line between the left and right entries.
13. Play the project to view your new credit roll in the Video Preview window.

pt Private Tutor: Reordering your credits

What happens in the event that you thought you finished your credits only to realize that you left a line out somewhere in the middle? Since no "reorder" buttons exist, you might think you have to do a lot of retyping, but a hidden solution exists. Insert a new line, and enter the desired information into it. Of course, the line is out of order since it was added to the end, but you need it in the middle. Select the new line and press **Ctrl+X** to cut the new line. Select the line you want to appear immediately after the new one in your credit roll and press **Ctrl+V** to paste the new line above the selected line.

pt Private Tutor: Creating credits externally

You can also use your favorite word processor or other application to compose your credits. When you're done, copy them from the other application and paste them into the Credit Roll generator. If you used tabs in your word processor, the credits are automatically formatted as Dual Items.

pt Private Tutor: Additional Media Generators

The Media Generators window contains other types of media generators that we haven't discussed in this module. Now that you know how media generators work, you're well equipped to get the most out of these additional generators. It's fun and informative to experiment with the different types of media generators and their various settings, and that's also a great way to learn more about them. In particular, work with the Checkerboard and Noise Generator media generators to create interesting backgrounds and graphic elements for your video projects.

Conclusion

As you learned in this module, a lot of power lies in generated media. You learned how to make solid color events that you can use as backgrounds. You also added gradients that can enhance the look of your video presentation and create interesting special effects. You now know how to create text overlays, and understand the power that media generators give you for making professional-looking scrolling credits quickly. One of the most significant things you learned in this module was how to use the keyframe controller and various parameter settings to make your generated media more dynamic. You will use the keyframe controller many times to enhance a wide variety of Vegas tools.

Exercises

1. True or false: You must install media generators separately in order to use them with Vegas.

2. What is the main advantage of using the Text/Background window to add media generators to a project?

    a. There are more available options.

    b. Presets are listed in alphabetical order.

    c. Thumbnails let you know what the preset looks like.

    d. Presets exist for Video Factory-compliant text.

3. True or false: In the preset thumbnails, a checkerboard pattern indicates transparency so that the better you can see the checkerboard, the more transparent the color will be.

4. True or false: The keyframe controller appears only in the Video Event FX window and thus is only useful for generated media.

5. Which of the following best describes a keyframe as used in the keyframe controller?

    a. The first frame of a new scene in your movie.

    b. The state of an object at a specific point in time.

    c. The most important frame in the movie.

    d. A special frame that helps the movie play more efficiently.

6. True or false: A gradient is the same thing as a blend.

7. Which of the following is not an option for the transition from one keyframe to the next in the keyframe timeline?

    a. Hold

    b. Smooth

    c. Fast

    d. Exponential

8. True or false: Credit rolls can only roll up.

9. True or false: Test patterns are used to make sure Vegas is working properly.

10. How many keyframes can you add to a single keyframe controller?

    a. The answer depends upon how much RAM you have on your computer.

    b. 10 for credit rolls and 15 for all other generators.

    c. Unlimited.

    d. 20.

11. Which of the following is not a valid gradient type in Vegas?

        a. Linear.

        b. Triangular.

        c. Elliptical.

        d. Rectangular.

12. True or false: In order to create a transparent portion in generated media, you must use the Checkerboard media generator.

13. Why is the safe zone important when generating text?

        a. Text positioned inside the safe zone will not be cut off on a TV monitor.

        b. Without the safe zone, your computer might crash when creating generated media.

        c. It keeps two adjacent events created with generated media from overlapping, thus causing video interference.

        d. It prevents you from inadvertently modifying the words entered into a text event.

Essays

1. Explain how you would use the keyframe controller to create a video sequence in which the background color starts out red, suddenly to blue after a few seconds, and transforms to yellow at an even pace over the next few seconds.

2. Describe the process you would go through to create a credit roll at the end of your movie that contains the following elements:

   - A headline
   - Two subheadings (on different lines)
   - 10 lines of text, each of which contains two columns

3. Describe how you would add a new subheading between the fifth and sixth line of two-column text.

Module 5: Navigation and zoom/view techniques

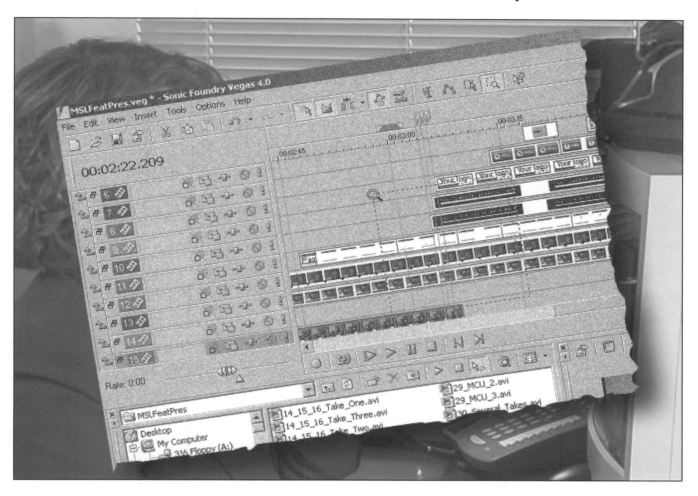

Back in Module 1, *The Vegas Interface*, you learned how to play and pause your project. In this module, you'll learn how to use the other transport buttons in Vegas. You'll create a loop region and explore its usefulness when editing a project. This module also discusses zoom and view techniques that help you find exact edit points in your project and make it easier to focus on a specific track or event.

In this module you'll do the following:

- Use the Vegas transport controls to play and navigate through your project.
- Master loop playback techniques.
- Learn how to resize tracks.
- Use zoom techniques to make it easier to work with specific areas of your project.

Lesson 1: Using the transport buttons

The transport bar, shown in **Figure 5.1**, hosts all of the buttons that enable you to navigate through, play, and record audio into your project. This lesson takes a close look at each of the buttons, with the exception of the **Record** button, which you learned about in Module 3.

Figure 5.1
The transport buttons are located at the bottom of the timeline.

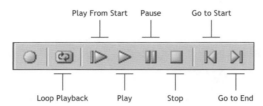

You've also already used the **Play** button, but let's quickly review what you know about it. Click the **Play** button (or press the spacebar) to begin project playback from the cursor position. The project begins to play back, and you see the cursor moving through the project. Notice that Vegas marks the point where the cursor started with a stationary vertical line. With the project still playing, click the **Play** button again. The cursor instantly returns to the starting point and continues playing from there.

With the project still playing, click the **Pause** button (or press the **Enter** key). This stops the cursor right where it is.

Like the **Pause** button, the **Stop** button also stops project playback. Play your project again. With the project playing, click the **Stop** button and notice that the project cursor jumps back to the starting point. Remember, the **Stop** button first stops playback and then automatically rewinds the project, while the **Pause** button stops playback and maintains the cursor position.

Task 1: Controlling project playback

In this task you'll use the **Play**, **Pause**, and **Stop** buttons to control the playback of your project.

1. Open *M05Task001.veg* in the *LessonFiles\Module05* folder on the companion CD.
2. Click the **Play** button.
3. As soon as you see the scene change from the bear to the eagle, click the **Pause** button. The cursor stops where it is.
4. Click the **Play** button again.
5. When the scene changes from the eagle to the hawk, click the **Stop** button. Now the cursor returns to the location where you started playback.
6. Keep this project open so you can use it in the next task.

pt Private Tutor: Spacebar behavior

Sonic Foundry has its roots deep in the digital audio world. From the beginning with all Sonic Foundry products, the spacebar has acted as the shortcut for the **Play** button when the project is stopped and for the **Stop** button when the project is playing. On the other hand, digital video editing packages have traditionally used the spacebar as a shortcut for the **Play** button when the project is stopped and for the **Pause** button when the project is playing. If you prefer the traditional video-editing behavior (play/pause), choose **Options | Preferences** to open the Preferences dialog. On the **General** tab, select the **Make spacebar and F12 Play/Pause instead of Play/Stop** check box. Click **OK** to close the Preferences dialog. The spacebar now behaves according to the traditional video-editing model.

The **Play From Start** button begins playback of your project from the beginning regardless of the cursor position. Click the **Play From Start** button. When you click the **Stop** button, the cursor returns to its position when you clicked **Play From Start** and not to the beginning of the project.

Task 2: Playing from the start

In this task, you'll learn the difference between the **Play** button and the **Play From Start** button.

1. If the project you worked on in the previous task is no longer open, open *M05Task001.veg* in the *LessonFiles\Module05* folder on the companion CD.
2. Click the **Play** button. The project begins playing from the current cursor position (between the bear and eagle clips if you completed Task 1).
3. Click the **Stop** button.
4. Click the **Play From Start** button (**Shift+Spacebar**). The project begins playing from the beginning without regard to the location of the cursor.
5. Click the **Stop** button. The cursor returns to its original position.
6. Keep this project open so you can use it in the next task.

Click the **Go to Start** button (**Ctrl+Home**) to return the cursor to the beginning of the project. If the project is playing when you click this button, the cursor returns to the beginning of the project and continues playing from there.

Click the **Go to End** button (**Ctrl+End**) to move the cursor to the end of the last event in the project. If the project is playing when you click this button, the cursor moves to the end of the project and continues playing from there (even though there is nothing more in the project to see or hear).

Task 3: Navigating to the beginning and end of the project

In this task, you'll use the **Go to Start** and **Go to End** buttons to navigate instantly to the start and end of your project.

1. If the project you worked on in the previous task is no longer open, open *M05Task001.veg* in the *\LessonFiles\Module05* folder on the companion CD.
2. Click the **Go to End** button. The cursor moves instantly to the end of the last event in the project.
3. Click the **Go to Start** button to move the cursor to the beginning of the project.
4. Leave this project open so you can use it in the next task.

Lesson 2: Using loop playback mode

The **Loop Playback** (refer to **Figure 5.1**) button toggles Vegas into and out of loop playback mode. In loop playback mode, you can define an area within your project that you want to play repeatedly again (known as looping the area) while you evaluate that section of the project and make edits or adjustments to it. To enter loop playback mode, click the **Loop Playback** button or press **Q**. Alternatively, choose **Options | Loop Playback**.

Above the time ruler at the top of the timeline, you can see the loop region indicator, shown in **Figure 5.2**. When not in loop playback mode, the bar is gray. When in loop playback mode, the bar is blue, and vertical lines run down through your project to identify the beginning and end of the loop region. You may also see blue shading in the timeline between the ends of the loop region. We'll talk more about this shading in Module 6, *Basic editing techniques*, Lesson 4, *Additional selection techniques*.

Figure 5.2

The Loop region turns blue when you enter loop playback mode.

Since you can adjust the length of the loop region, it may not appear to be a bar as in **Figure 5.2**. It may look like only one yellow triangle at the beginning of the timeline, or like two triangles next to each other. Both of these cases indicate that the loop region is too narrow to see. To adjust the length of the loop region, drag one of the yellow triangles left or right. Double-click an event to set the loop region to the exact length of the event. To move the loop region without changing its length, drag the bar.

Task 4: Setting up loop playback

This task shows you how to enter loop playback mode and adjust the loop region to the length you want.

1. If the project you worked on in the previous task is no longer open, open *M05Task001.veg* in the *LessonFiles\Module05* folder on the companion CD.
2. Double-click the event that holds the eagle clip. This sets the loop region to the length of that event.
3. Click anywhere on the timeline and notice that clicking in the timeline does not change the length of the loop region (although it does make the blue shading disappear from the timeline).
4. Click the **Loop Playback** button to enter loop playback mode.
5. Drag the yellow triangle at the left end of the loop region to the left to make the loop region longer, then right to make it shorter. Do the same with the yellow triangle on the right end of the bar.
6. Drag the middle of the loop region to move it.
7. Leave this project open so you can work more with it in the following task.

With Vegas in loop playback mode, the project plays normally until it reaches the end of the loop region. At that point, the cursor returns to the beginning of the loop region and continues to play. This cycle—or loop—continues until you stop playback or turn off loop playback mode. If the cursor is already located after the loop region when you click the **Play** button, loop playback mode has no effect on playback since the cursor never reaches the end of the loop region.

Task 5: Playing your project in loop playback mode

In this task, you'll play your project in loop playback mode to see how you can continually play a section of your project while working on it.

1. If the project you worked on in the previous task is no longer open, repeat Task 4, *Setting up loop playback.*
2. Click in the timeline before the loop region to place the cursor.
3. Click the **Play** button. Let the project play through the loop region to see how it starts over when it reaches the end.
4. After you've seen it play through the region a couple of times (and with the project still playing), click the **Loop Playback** button to turn off loop playback mode. When the cursor reaches the end of the region, it plays right through since you are no longer in loop playback mode.
5. Close the project without saving your work.

Lesson 3: Keyboard shortcuts and focus

Now that we've talked about using shortcuts to play, stop, and pause your project, we need to turn our attention to focus for a moment. In this lesson, you'll learn how the focus of the interface affects keyboard shortcuts.

You know already that the Vegas screen is divided into several sections. When you click in a specific section, that section gains focus, or becomes the active portion of the interface. Vegas usually provides some visual cue so you can identify the section of the screen that has focus. For instance, when the timeline has focus, the cursor flashes. When a track header has focus, a small line at the bottom of the track icon flashes. When the Explorer window has focus, you'll generally see an item in the folder/file list selected or with a dotted line around it.

Make sure you know which section of the screen has focus, because keyboard shortcuts affect the portion of the Vegas window that has focus. For example, the spacebar has different functions depending upon which area of the screen has focus. If the timeline or track list has focus, the spacebar works as the shortcut for the **Play/Stop** buttons in the timeline. However, if the Explorer window has focus with a file selected, the spacebar works as the shortcut for the **Start Preview/Stop Preview** buttons.

Task 6: Experimenting with focus

In this task, you'll see how the function of the spacebar depends upon which window has focus.

1. Create a new project.
2. In the Explorer window, browse to the *SampleMedia**Video* folder on the companion CD.
3. Add *eaglefly2.avi* to the timeline. Notice that the cursor flashes within the timeline to indicate that the timeline currently has focus.
4. Press the spacebar. Since the timeline has focus, this shortcut starts/stops playback on the timeline.
5. Select *hawkMed.avi* in the Explorer window.
6. Press the spacebar. Instead of stopping project playback, this time *hawkMed.avi* begins to preview. Since the Explorer window has focus, the spacebar works as the shortcut for Start/Stop Preview.

Private Tutor: A shortcut for play no matter which window has focus

pt Since playing your project is obviously such an important function, Vegas provides a couple of shortcuts to start playback regardless of focus. Press **Ctrl+Spacebar** or **F12** to play/stop the project even if the timeline doesn't have focus. You might even want to get into the habit of using **Ctrl+Spacebar** to play your project whether the timeline has focus or not so you don't have to worry about it.

Lesson 4: Controlling project view (zoom levels)

In the next Module, *Basic Editing Techniques*, you'll learn some of the most common methods you can use to edit your video. As you work with your video projects, you'll find that sometimes you would like to concentrate on an event or an edit point. In this lesson, you'll learn to use the various zoom tools in Vegas to change the magnification of your project.

In Vegas, you can zoom horizontally (called "zoom in/out time") and vertically (called "zoom in/out track height"). Both zoom methods play important roles in your editing, and several methods exist for zooming in both directions— either individually or simultaneously.

The Zoom tool provides a familiar zoom method for anyone who has used graphics software. You can access the Zoom tool in these ways:

- Choose **Edit | Editing Tool | Zoom**.
- Click the **Zoom Tool** button in the Vegas toolbar (see **Figure 5.3**).
- Click the **Zoom Tool** button in the lower-right-hand corner of the timeline (see **Figure 5.3**).

Figure 5.3
There are several ways to access the Zoom tool.

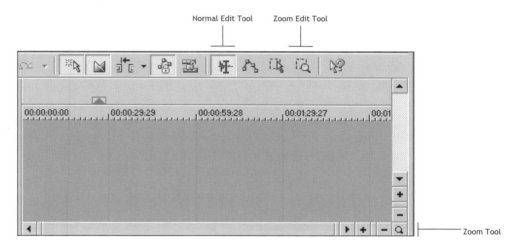

Click anywhere within the timeline with the Zoom tool to zoom out as far as possible. This makes every track in your project as small vertically as possible (known as minimizing each track), and resizes the project horizontally to fit the entire project in the visible area of the timeline.

To zoom in, select the Zoom tool, and then drag around an area in the timeline. This enlarges the selected area as much as possible (as dictated by the size of the visible timeline). When you're done zooming, click the **Normal Edit Tool** button, shown in **Figure 5.3** (or choose **Edit | Editing Tool | Normal Edit**) and resume working on your edits.

pt **Private Tutor: Switching between edit tools**

Choose **Edit | Editing Tool** to view the list of available tools. You can use keyboard shortcuts to change from one tool to another. Press **D** on your keyboard to switch to the next editing tool in the list. Press **Shift+D** to switch to the previous tool in the list. Press **Ctrl+D** to return to the Normal Edit Tool regardless of the currently active tool.

Task 7: Using the Zoom tool

This task shows you how to zoom in time and zoom in track height simultaneously with the Zoom tool. You'll also see an example of when zooming into your project is critical for proper editing.

1. Open *M05Task007.veg in the LessonFiles\Module05* folder on the companion CD.
2. Notice the video events in track 1. When your project is zoomed far out, they look as though they touch one another. Click the **Play** button to view the project. If you watch closely, you'll notice a quick flash of black in your Video Preview window between the bear and eagle events. We'll zoom in to find the problem.
3. Click the **Zoom Tool** button.
4. Drag from the right edge of the bear event to just past the left edge of the eagle event. In other words, create a zoom area that includes the spot where the first clip ends and the second clip begins.
5. When you release the mouse button, you zoom in instantly. At this increased zoom level, you can see that the two events do not actually touch. The gray area between the two events is the blank track showing through the gap between the two events, and you see this as a black flash when you preview the project.
6. With the Zoom tool still selected, click anywhere on the timeline to zoom all the way out again.
7. Click the **Normal Edit Tool** button.
8. Close this project without saving your changes.

To zoom in or out on the timeline (horizontally), use the zoom time controls located in the lower-right corner of the timeline. Click the **Zoom In Time** button (**Up Arrow**) to zoom in step by step, or click and hold the button to zoom all the way in. Click the **Zoom Out Time** button (**Down Arrow**) to zoom out step by step, or click and hold the button to zoom all the way out.

Drag the bar between the **Zoom In Time** and the **Zoom Out Time** buttons to the left and right to zoom in and out horizontally. This control provides a quick way to zoom in and out in large increments.

When you use the zoom time controls, the focal point of the zoom is the cursor so that as you zoom in, the cursor always remains visible on your screen. Therefore, these controls are most useful when (as in the task below) you click to place the cursor at or very near the exact point in your project you want to inspect at a different zoom level.

Task 8: Using the Zoom In/Out Time buttons

In this task, you'll use the **Zoom In Time** and **Zoom Out Time** buttons to change the horizontal magnification of your project.

1. Open *M05Task007.veg* in the *LessonFiles\Module05* folder on the companion CD.
2. Click in the timeline to place the cursor close to the point where the bear event ends and the eagle event begins.
3. Click the **Zoom In Time** button until you can see the space between the two events.
4. Click and hold the **Zoom Out Time** button until the project zooms all the way out again.
5. Drag the bar between the **Zoom In Time** and **Zoom Out Time** buttons to the left until you can see the space between the two events again.
6. Drag the bar between the **Zoom Time In** and **Zoom Time Out** buttons to the right until the project is zoomed all the way out.
7. Keep this project open so that you can work with it more in the next task.

Private Tutor: Zooming with the mouse wheel

If you have a mouse with a mouse wheel, hover over the timeline and use the mouse wheel to quickly zoom in or out.

The horizontal scroll box at the bottom of the timeline also functions as a zoom time tool. It acts differently from the zoom time controls we just discussed in that it does not use the cursor as the focal point of the zoom. Instead, when you use the scroll box to zoom, the focal point becomes the earliest visible spot in the timeline or the latest visible spot in the timeline as described below.

To use the scroll box to zoom in and out, drag either end of the scroll box. If dragging the left end of the scroll box, Vegas uses the latest visible spot in the timeline as the focal point. Drag right to zoom in or left to zoom out. If dragging the right end of the scroll box, Vegas uses the earliest visible spot in the timeline as the focal point. Drag left to zoom in, and right to zoom out. Finally, double-click the scroll box to zoom all the way out.

Task 9: Using the horizontal scroll box to zoom

This task shows you how the scroll box functions as a zoom tool.

1. If the project you worked on in the previous task is no longer open, open *M05Task007.veg* in the *LessonFiles\Module05* folder on the companion CD.
2. Drag the left edge of the scroll box to the right to zoom in as far as you can. Notice that since the last visible spot on the timeline contains no events, eventually you zoom in so far that no event is visible.
3. Double-click the scroll box to zoom out completely.
4. Drag the right edge of the scroll box to the left until you've zoomed in as far as possible. This time, the earliest visible spot in the timeline (in this case, the beginning of the project) serves as the focal point.
5. Double-click the scroll box to zoom out completely.
6. Keep this project open so that you can work with it in the next task.

pt Private Tutor: Zooming in other places

You'll see zoom controls appear in other windows within Vegas in addition to the timeline. For instance, the keyframe controllers have similar zoom tools. Look for zoom controls whenever you find yourself wishing you could get a closer look at what you're working on. If you wish you could zoom in or out, you'll probably find zoom controls to let you do just that.

Use the zoom track height controls when you want to make all tracks in your project taller or shorter. Click the **Zoom In Track Height** button repeatedly to increase track height one step at a time. Click and hold the **Zoom In Track Height** button to increase track height of all tracks until the selected track occupies the entire height of the timeline. Click the **Zoom Out Track Height** button repeatedly to decrease track height one step at a time. Click and hold the **Zoom Out Track Height** button to zoom out completely.

Drag the bar between the **Zoom In Track Height** and **Zoom Out Track Height** buttons up to increase track height and down to decrease track height. This control provides a quick way to zoom in and out in large increments.

If not zoomed out completely already, double-click the vertical scroll box to zoom out completely. If zoomed out completely, double-click the vertical scroll box to return all tracks to the default track height.

Task 10: Zooming track height

In this task, you'll change track height with the **Zoom Track Height** controls and the vertical scroll box.

1. If the project you worked on in the previous task is no longer open, open *M05Task007.veg* in the *LessonFiles\Module05* folder on the companion CD.
2. Click the **Zoom In Track Height** button to increase the track height. Click and hold the button to increase the track height until the selected track occupies the entire height of the timeline.
3. Drag the bar between the **Zoom In Track Height** and **Zoom Out Track Height** buttons down to decrease the height of each track to the smallest height possible.
4. Double-click the vertical scroll box to return each track to the default track height.

Conclusion

In this module, you learned how to get at the details of your project by using the zoom tools. You also learned how to quickly navigate from one end of your project to the other. You used loop playback mode and discovered how this can be helpful when working on a specific section of your project. You also learned how focus affects the behavior of shortcut keys. You'll use these techniques often, so mastering them now will help you quickly increase your productivity.

Exercises

1. Which of the following best describes the difference between the **Play** button and the **Play From Start** button?

   a. You can click the Play button at any time, while you cannot click the Play From Start button while the project is playing.

   b. The Play button adjusts the position of the cursor; the Play From Start button does not.

   c. Double-clicking the Play button plays the project at double speed, but double-clicking the Play From Start button has no effect.

   d. The Play button begins project playback from the current cursor position, but the Play From Start button begins playback from the start of the project regardless of the location of the cursor.

2. True or false: The spacebar must always act as a toggle between **Play** and **Stop**.

3. True or false: There is no functional difference between the **Pause** and **Stop** buttons.

4. Which of the following describes the usefulness of loop playback mode?

   a. You can play an area of your project repeatedly without having to repeatedly click **Play**.

   b. You can use audio loops in your project to create special sound effects.

   c. You can create a movie that can loop endlessly.

   d. Loop playback mode ensures that the media you use to build the current project can also be used in a later project.

5. True or false: You can drag the yellow triangles on either end of the loop region to adjust the length of the loop region.

6. True or false: Once you define the loop region, its position cannot be changed.

7. Which of the following describes a situation in which the loop region has absolutely no effect on playback of the project?

   a. You hold the Ctrl key when you click the **Play** button (the Ctrl key overrides Play Looped mode).

   b. You start project playback with the **Play From Start** button instead of the **Play** button.

   c. The cursor is currently located after the loop region has ended, and you click the **Play** button to begin project playback.

   d. The cursor is currently located before the loop region has begun, and you click the **Play** button to begin project playback.

8. Why is focus important when using keyboard shortcuts?

   a. Some keystrokes produce different results depending on which window has focus.

   b. Focus makes your video look clearer to the viewer.

   c. Assigning focus "pairs" enables you to use a single keyboard shortcut to accomplish two or more functions simultaneously.

   d. Focus has nothing to do with keyboard shortcuts.

9. True or false: Because the play function is so important, you can press **F12** to play your project no matter which window has focus.

10. Which two of the following describe ways to zoom into or out of the timeline?

    a. Zoom In/Out Time.

    b. Zoom In/Out Horizontally.

    c. Zoom In/Out Events.

    d. Zoom In/Out Track Height.

11. Draw a line from the keyboard shortcut to the action it performs:

    a. Spacebar   Play regardless of focus

    b. Ctrl+Spacebar   Zoom In Time

    c. Up Arrow   Loop playback mode

    d. Q   Play/Stop

    e. Ctrl+D   Select the Normal Edit Tool

Essays

1. Describe the difference between the results of clicking the **Stop** button and the results of clicking the **Pause** button.

2. Describe a situation in which you would make use of loop playback mode. How could you use the zoom techniques you learned in this module in conjunction with loop playback mode?

Module 6: Basic editing techniques

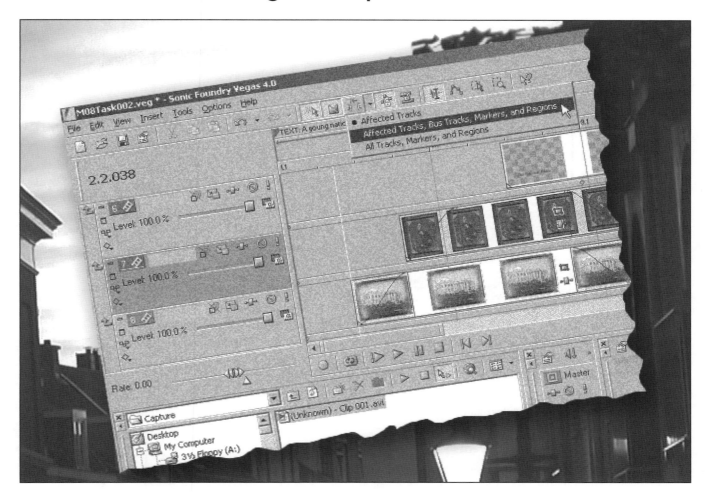

So far, you've learned many ways to add media files to your projects. You've seen that not only can you add a variety of media files, but you can also create your own media using media generators, Sonic Foundry Video Capture, and audio recording. The real strength of Vegas, however, is what you can do with the media files once you've added them to the timeline. This module focuses on the basic editing techniques that you use to build exactly the video or audio project you envision. We call them basic, but there's a lot of power in the techniques we discuss here.

In this module you'll learn how to do the following:

- Make simple and complex selections on the timeline.
- Reposition events.
- Edge trim events.
- Cut, copy, paste, and delete events.
- Use ripple editing techniques
- Split one event into two or more.
- Use markers and regions to organize your work.

Lesson 1: Selecting events

Throughout this module, you'll perform a number of operations on events in the timeline to create the exact edits you want, but before you can edit events, you must select them. As you'll see in this lesson and Lesson 4, *Additional selection techniques*, there are several different selection scenarios. You'll see that sometimes the same editing technique achieves different results depending upon the selection you make. These selection techniques are therefore quite important because once they become second nature to you, you'll more fully understand the wide variety of options you have available at virtually every editing decision point in your project. In this lesson, you'll learn how to select one or more events in preparation for editing.

To select an event on the timeline, click it. An unselected audio event has a white background as shown in **Figure 6.1**, and the waveform within the event is the color of the track icon in the event's track header. When you select an audio event, Vegas changes the event's background color to match the color of the track icon and changes the color of the waveform to lighter shade of that color.

Figure 6.1
Unselected events have white backgrounds.

The background of a selected video event also changes to match the color of the track icon in the track header. You can see the background of the video event along the top and bottom edges of the event (and before and after each thumbnail if the event is long enough to hold more than one thumbnail).

To select a different event, click it. The previously selected event becomes deselected, while the new event is simultaneously selected. To deselect all events, click anywhere in the timeline that does not contain an event.

Task 1: Selecting single events

In this task, you'll select an audio event and then a video event. You'll compare the look of the selected events to copies of the same events that are not selected.

1. Open *M06Task001.veg* in the *LessonFiles\Module06* folder on the companion CD. Track 1 holds two events that contain the same piece of audio media. Track 2 holds two events that contain the same piece of video media. Notice that both video events look the same, as do the two audio events.
2. Click one of the audio events to select it. Its background changes to red, and the waveform changes to a pale shade of the same red.
3. Click one of the video events to select it. This deselects the audio event you selected in Step 2. Compare the background of the selected event (which is now blue) with the background of the unselected video event (which remains white).
4. Click a blank area of the timeline to deselect all events in the project.

pt **Private Tutor: Repositioning the cursor without deselecting events**

As you saw in the previous task, you can click anywhere in the timeline that does not contain an event to deselect events. Sometimes, however, this presents a bit of a problem because often you'll want to reposition the cursor without losing your selection. To accomplish this, click the blank area right above the time ruler (the area that holds the loop region). The cursor moves to the point at which you click and any selected events remain selected.

You can select several events at the same time and then apply an edit to all of those events. You can use several different techniques to select multiple events. Hold the **Ctrl** or **Shift** key while clicking events to select more than one event on the timeline.

Vegas also provides a quick way to select an event and every event that comes after it in the same track: right-click the first event you want to select and choose **Select Events to End** from the shortcut menu. This is one way to deal with situations in which you decide that an event should occur at a different point in your project, but that all the events that follow it should maintain their current relationship to the original event. In this case, select all the events and move the first one to the desired point in the project. All of the other selected events move accordingly. (You'll learn how to move events in Lesson 2 of this module, *Moving events*.)

Task 2: Selecting multiple events

In this task, you'll use the two techniques you've learned for selecting more than one event at a time.

1. Open *M06Task002.veg* in the *LessonFiles\Module06* folder on the companion CD.
2. Click the first audio event to select it.
3. Hold the **Ctrl** key and click the last audio event to add it to the selection.
4. If you're not still holding down the Ctrl key, do so again now. Click the second video event in track 2 (the eagle event in the middle of the project) to add it to the selection.
5. Click a blank area of the timeline to deselect all selected events.
6. Click the second audio event to select it.
7. Hold the Shift key and click the hawk event in track 3. This adds the hawk event and every event between it and the second audio event (selected in Step 6) to the selection. Notice that *between* the events means horizontally across the timeline and vertically across tracks.
8. Click a blank area of the timeline to deselect all events.
9. Right-click the second audio event and choose **Select Events to End** from the shortcut menu. This selects the second event and every event that occurs after it in the same track. The first audio event remains unselected.
10. Click a blank area of the timeline to deselect all events. Keep this project open so you can use it again in the next task.

pt Private Tutor: Combining two selection techniques

You've learned two ways to select more than one event at a time. You can also combine these two techniques to select all events from a certain point on the timeline to the end of the project even if the events are on different tracks. To do this, first use the Ctrl+click method to select the first event in each track that you want to select. Now, right-click any one of the selected events and choose **Select Events to End** from the shortcut menu. This selects all of the events in the project that follow each of the selected events.

The Selection Edit tool provides another familiar way to select more than one event at a time, by drawing a selection rectangle anywhere in the timeline. To use the Selection Edit tool, choose **Edit | Editing Tool | Selection**, or click the **Selection Edit Tool** button, shown in **Figure 6.2**.

Figure 6.2
Click the **Selection Edit Tool** button to use the Selection Edit tool.

Selection Edit Tool

The Selection Edit tool has three states. In the default state, you define the selection area rectangle in a free-form manner. In other words, you define the length and width of the rectangle. In the second state, you control only the width of the rectangle; the height of the rectangle always stretches across every track in the project. Use this mode to quickly select all of the events within a certain time range. The third state allows you to control only the height of the rectangle; the width of the rectangle stretches across the entire length of the project. Use this mode to quickly select every event on a track or multiple tracks.

To rotate through the three selection states, click and drag to begin defining a rectangle in the default free-form state. Continue to hold the left mouse button, and then click the right mouse button. The first click changes to the horizontal-adjustment-only state, the next click changes to the vertical-adjustment-only state, and the third click returns to the free-form state.

Task 3: Using the Selection Edit tool

This task shows you how to use the various states of the Selection Edit tool to define a selection area.

1. If the file from the previous task is no longer open, open *M06Task002.veg* in the *LessonFiles\Module06* folder on the companion CD.
2. Click the **Selection Edit Tool** button.
3. Click the second audio event, and hold the mouse button while dragging the selection rectangle down and to the right until you reach the hawk event in track 3, then release the mouse button. Notice that this selects all events that fell at least partially within the selection area you defined (which does not include the first event on track 1 or track 2).
4. Click a blank area of the timeline to deselect all selected events.
5. Click the second audio event and hold the mouse button while dragging the selection rectangle down and to the right until you reach the blank area between the second and third video events on track 2. Do not release the mouse button.
6. While still holding the mouse button, click the right mouse button. This changes the state of the Selection Edit tool so you can now change only the width of the selection rectangle. Notice that this adds the bear event in track 3 to the selection.
7. While still holding down the left mouse button, click the right mouse button again. This changes the state of the Selection Edit tool so you can now change only the height of the selection rectangle. Notice that this removes the event in track 3 from the selection and adds every event in tracks 1 and 2.
8. Click the **Normal Edit Tool**.

pt **Private Tutor: Adding or removing events from a selection "on the fly"**

When making a selection with the Selection Edit tool, you are not committed to the events you include in the selection as long as you continue to hold the mouse button. With the mouse button down, any event the selection area touches becomes selected, but as soon as you back the selection off so that it no longer touches an event, that event becomes deselected. This enables you to make exactly the selection you want without having to "shoot perfectly" the first time you drag the selection area rectangle.

A final selection technique allows you to quickly select all of the events in your project, no matter where they are in the timeline. To do so, click anywhere in the timeline and choose **Edit | Select All** or press **Ctrl+A**.

pt **Private Tutor: Grouping events**

You can group events so you don't disrupt the relationship between them. When you add a video clip that contains audio to your project, the video and audio events are grouped. To group selected events, right-click one of them and choose **Group | Create New** from the shortcut menu.

Lesson 2: Moving events

Rarely (if ever) will you be perfectly content to leave your events exactly where you originally dropped them onto the timeline. Once you've selected an event, you can move it to the desired position in your project. In this lesson, you'll learn how to move an event to exactly the right spot in the timeline.

Moving an event on the timeline couldn't be easier. Simply drag the event to the left or right to move it later or earlier in the project. When you have it positioned where you want it, release the mouse button. You can also drag an event to any position within a different track, or even drag the event to a blank spot in the timeline to instantly create a new track to hold the event at that point in the timeline.

As the left edge of an event approaches one of the gray grid lines in the timeline, the event snaps (jumps) to that grid line. By default, the left edge of an event snaps to several objects (which we'll call *snap points*) in the timeline including grid lines, the cursor, the right edge of another event, markers, region markers, and the beginning and end of a time selection. (You'll learn more about time selections in Lesson 5, *Additional selection techniques*, and more about markers and regions in Lesson 8, *Markers and regions*.)

Snapping can help you position your event at an exact location in your project. For instance, when one event snaps to another, you can rest assured that no space exists between the two events that might cause a momentary flash of black in your final video. Without snapping, you'd have to zoom in to make sure that no space existed between the two events, which would become very time consuming (and annoying) over the course of a long editing session.

As useful as snapping usually is, sometimes it can get in your way. For instance, if you're trying to move an event just a small amount and you get too close to a snap point, your event might jump past where you want to place it and land at the snap point instead. In these cases, you might want to turn snapping off. Choose **Options | Enable Snapping** to toggle snapping on or off.

You can also suspend snapping for grid lines and/or markers while keeping snapping on for all other snap points. To toggle snapping to the grid on or off, choose **Options | Snap to Grid**, or choose **Options | Snap to Markers** to toggle snapping to your markers on or off.

Task 4: Moving events

In this task, you'll move events and experiment with snap objects.

1. Open *M06Task004.veg* in the *LessonFiles\Module06* folder on the companion CD.
2. Click between the two grid lines that lie between the two events.
3. Drag the bear event to the left. Notice that when you get close enough to the first grid line between the two events, the event you're moving snaps to the grid line.
4. Drag the bear event farther to the left until its left edge snaps to the cursor, which you placed between the grid lines in Step 2.
5. Drag the bear event to the left until its left edge snaps to the right edge of the eagle event.
6. Drag the bear event to the right until you have a good deal of space between the two events.
7. Click to place the cursor at the right end of the eagle event.
8. Drag the bear event into a blank area of the timeline. This creates a new track to hold the event.
9. Drag the bear event until it snaps to the cursor. You've just learned to use the cursor as a snap point to quickly line up the beginning of an event on one track to the end of an event on another track.

Private Tutor: Quantize to Frames

pt The **Quantize to Frames** feature works much like snapping. With **Quantize to Frames** turned on, Vegas does not allow you to create an edit in the middle of a video frame on the timeline. Your events and cursor placements always snap to the nearest frame boundary. In some instances, you don't want to use the **Quantize to Frames** feature (for example, the feature is not necessary in most audio-only projects). To toggle **Quanitze to Frames** on or off, choose **Options | Quantize to Frames**. Unless you're zoomed quite far into your timeline, you probably won't even notice the results of this feature when you're moving events.

Private Tutor: Temporarily overriding snapping

pt You can temporarily override snapping (and **Quantize to Frames**) when you want to position an event without being influenced by snap points. To do so, after you begin to drag the event, hold down the **Shift** key to override snapping.

Although moving events is quite easy (as you just learned), things become slightly more complicated when you want to change the sequence of events on the timeline as when you are assembling a rough storyboard edit in your project. For example, if you want to change the order of events from *1, 2, 3, 4* to *1, 4, 2, 3.* , you need to first move events 2 and 3 out of the way to make room for event 4 after event 1, then move event 4 into place, and finally move events 2 and 3 into place behind event 4.

You can use the techniques you just learned to accomplish the task, but event shuffling provides a more efficient one-step method. To use event shuffling to accomplish the edit in the example mentioned above, use your right mouse button to drag event 4 until the mouse points to 2. Release the right mouse button and choose **Shuffle Events** from the shortcut menu as shown in **Figure 6.3**. This moves event into its new position and shuffles every event that follows its new position (on the same track) toward the end of the project to make room for the moved event. This is a great way to do a quick rough edit so you can view the video to see how it flows before you begin the detail editing.

Figure 6.3
The **Shuffle Events** command is found in the shortcut menu when you right-drag an event.

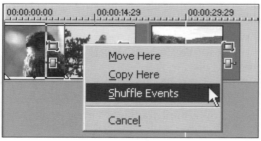

Task 5: Event shuffling

In this task you'll use event shuffling to quickly rearrange the order of both video and audio events.

1. Open *M06Task005.veg* in the *LessonFiles\Module06* folder on the companion CD. Notice that the event order for the video track is eagle, bear, hawk.
2. Use your right mouse button to drag the hawk event over the top of the eagle event.
3. Release the mouse and choose **Shuffle Events** from the shortcut menu. The hawk event moves to the first position, and the eagle and bear events shuffle to the right to make room for the hawk.
4. Right-click and drag the bear event over the top of the eagle event and choose **Shuffle Events** to make the bear event the second event and the eagle the third event. Your event order is now hawk, bear, eagle.
5. Shuffle the second audio event to make it the first audio event.
6. Close the project without saving your changes.

Lesson 4: Edge trimming an event

Sometimes you don't want to include an entire media clip in your project. In this lesson, you'll learn to edge trim events to cut out or add portions of media at the beginning and/or end.

At first glance, edge trimming seems to simply make the event longer or shorter. This is only a partially accurate explanation of what happens when you perform an edge trim. It may help to imagine that when you add a media clip to the timeline, that media clip has a certain length and a certain position on the timeline, as indicated by the event that Vegas creates to hold the media. By default, the length of the event matches the length of the media clip it holds. However, you can edge trim the event so the two lengths no longer match. Keep in mind that you are changing the length of the event, but *not the length of the media the event holds*. The original media is always there and its length never changes. What does change when you edge trim an event is the amount of the media you choose to show inside the event that holds it. Think of an event as a window through which shows some or all of the media file on the other side.

To edge trim an event, hover your mouse over the right or left edge of the event. The pointer changes to the edge trim icon, which is ⊡ if you're trimming the left edge of the event or ⊡ if you're edge trimming the right edge. The distinction between these two icons is particularly important when you're trimming the edge of an event that sits right next to another event because it indicates which event you are trimming. When you see the appropriate edge trim icon, drag the edge of the event until you have covered or revealed as much of the media within the event as you want.

Private Tutor: Snapping and edge trimming

pt The snapping feature that we discussed in the previous lesson also affects edge trimming. As you drag the edge of an event, it snaps to all of the normal snap points. To temporarily override snapping, hold the **Shift** key after you begin edge trimming.

When you trim the edge to make the event smaller, it is easy to see that you cut out a piece of the media. For example, when you trim the beginning of the event, you cut out the beginning of the media within the event.

On the other hand, when you extend the edge to make the event longer, a couple of possibilities exist. If you previously trimmed the event, you can uncover the media that you cut out earlier. However, you could also make the event longer than the media it holds. By default, Vegas fills in the extra length of the event with repetitions (or loops) of the media. If you don't want the media to loop within the event, right-click the event and choose **Switches | Loop** to turn off looping. With looping off, you cannot extend the left edge of the event past the beginning of the media, and when you extend the right edge past the end of the media, Vegas repeats the last frame of the media, creating a freeze frame, to fill in the extra event time.

Task 6: Edge trimming events

In this task, you'll become familiar with edge trimming events to edit out portions of media that you don't want to appear in your movie. You'll also explore the results of extending an event so that it is longer than the media it holds.

1. Open *M06Task006.veg* in the *LessonFiles\Module06* folder on the companion CD.
2. Look at the waveform for the audio event in track 1 and notice that at about the 1:14:27 mark (look at the time ruler) the audio gets quieter as indicated by the smaller waveform that starts at that point. Later, it gets loud again and then fades out to end. Click to place your cursor just before the point that the music quiets down and click the **Play** button to listen to the end of the event.
3. At 1:21:05 there is a break that could serve as the end of the song. Press **Ctrl+G** to highlight the time value in the **Cursor Position** box.
4. Type 1.21.05, then press the **Enter** key to move the cursor to that time.
5. Hover your mouse over the right edge of the audio event until you see the edge trim icon.
6. Drag the right edge of the event to the left until it snaps to the project cursor.

7. Listen to the new ending for the event.
8. Extend the right edge of the event back out to the right, and notice that the original media is still available. It did not go away when you trimmed it in Step 6.
9. Click to place your cursor just before the video clip on track 2.
10. Click the **Play** button, and watch as the bear starts off-camera and then walks into the picture. Click the **Stop** button.
11. Trim the left edge of the bear event. Watch the thumbnail, which updates as you drag the edge to the right. Stop when the bear is fully visible in the thumbnail.
12. Position the cursor before the event and play the project again. You've successfully edited your video so that it starts with the bear fully on screen.
13. Trim the right edge of the video clip until it lasts for as long as the music in track 1 lasts.
14. Notice the triangular indentations at the top of the event (see **Figure 6.4**). These indicate where one loop of the video ends and the next begins (and they are also snap points). Play the video and notice that the bear clip repeats several times until the end of the event.

Figure 6.4
Triangular indentations indicate that the media loops in order to fill the entire event.

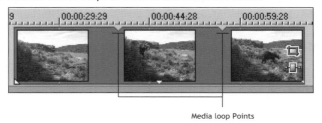

Media loop Points

15. Right-click the bear event and choose **Switches | Loop** from the shortcut menu. This turns looping off. Notice that most of the indentations at the top of the event disappear. The one remaining indentation indicates the end of the original media and the point at which the freeze frame begins.
16. Play the project and notice that after the media plays entirely, the last frame remains on screen until the event ends.

Now that you know how trimming works, you can use keyboard trimming to speed your editing process significantly. With keyboard trimming, you can edge edit events without reaching for your mouse. First, make sure the **Num Lock** feature on your keyboard is engaged. Then, click the event that you want to edit and press **7** on your numeric pad. This selects the first the event edge to the left of the cursor. A red bracket identifies the selected event edge. If two events touch, you can determine which event's edge is selected in two ways. First, the event itself changes colors to indicate that it is selected (exactly like it does if you click to select it), and second the tails of the red selection bracket point in the direction of the selected event. Press the **7** key again to choose the next event edge to the left of the currently selected edge. If the currently selected edge is the left edge of the event, the selection bracket jumps to the right edge of the event to the left of the currently selected event. In the same way, press the **9** key to select the next edge to the right of the currently selected edge (or to the right of the cursor if no edge is currently selected).

Now that you've selected the event edge that you want to edit, press **4** on your numeric pad. This trims the selected edge to the left one screen pixel per each press. Depending upon your zoom ratio, one screen pixel may represent several video frames. Press the **6** key to trim the edge to the right by one screen pixel per key press. The Video Preview window updates as the cursor moves, so you can press and hold the keys and watch for the exact spot to which you want to trim.

When you get close to the spot to which you want to trim the event, press **1** on your numeric keypad to trim the event to the left again. This time, however, you trim one frame at a time regardless of your zoom ratio. Press the **3** key to trim one frame to the right. The **4** and **6** keys enable you to get close to the right spot by taking larger jumps through your video (again, depending upon your zoom level), while the **1** and **3** keys let you zero in on the exact frame to which you want to edit.

When you're done trimming the current event edge, use the **7** and **9** keys to move to the next event edge that you'd like to trim. Note that while you can play your project when in edge trimming mode, the Video Preview window does not update. Instead, it continues to show the edge being trimmed. When you're completely done edge trimming, press the **5** key to exit edge trimming mode.

Some computer keyboards don't have a separate numeric pad (although many laptops have one built into the main keyboard—press the **Fn** key to access it), but you can still take advantage of enhanced trimming if you have a mouse with a wheel on it. To select the next event edge to the left without a numeric keypad, click the event you want to edit, and then choose **Edit | Select | Select Event Start** (or press the **[** key) to select the event edge to the left of the cursor, or **Edit | Select | Select Event End** (or the **]** key) to select the event edge to the right of the cursor. Now, hold **Ctrl+Shift** and roll the mouse wheel up (away from you) to edit to the left, or down (toward you) to edit to the right by screen pixels. This action emulates pressing the **4** and **6** keys on the numeric keypad. Hold down **Alt+Ctrl+Shift** and roll the mouse wheel up to edit one frame at a time to the left, and down to edit one frame at a time to the right. This action emulates pressing the **1** and the **3** keys.

Task 7: Keyboard trimming

In this task you'll use the keyboard to edge edit an event.

1. Open *M06Task007.veg* in the *LessonFiles\Module06* folder on the companion CD.
2. Click on the bear event to select it.
3. Make sure the **Num Lock** feature is active on your keyboard and press the **7** key to select the left edge of the bear event.
4. Press the **6** key to edge edit the event until the bear's head is visible in the Video Preview window.
5. Press the **4** key to trim it back until only the bear's nose is in the frame.
6. Press the **9** key as many times as necessary to select the right edge of the eagle event.
7. Press the **4** key until the eagle is seated on the limb, wings folded. Use the 1 and 3 keys to find the exact frame just before the eagle unfolds his wings. This edits out the portion of the event where the eagle flies away.
8. Click the audio event in the second track.
9. Use the keyboard techniques you've learned to trim the silence off the end of the audio event.
10. Close the project without saving your changes.

pt Private Tutor: Trimming heads and tails

Recall our discussion of heads and tails from Module 3, *Adding media to your project: advanced methods*, Lesson 1, *Capturing Video*. You can now use these edge-trimming techniques to remove the heads and tails from the video that you shoot with your camcorder and capture for use in your Vegas projects. Of course, if you later decide that you would like to use the heads and tails, simply extend the event to include them again.

Lesson 5: Additional selection techniques

In Lesson 1, you learned how to select events. While the ability to select events is an indispensable editing tool, it's not the only way to make selections in the timeline. In this lesson, you'll learn two additional selection techniques: time selections and combination time and event selections. You'll use the three different selection techniques depending upon the editing results you want to achieve. This lesson shows you these additional selection techniques. In the next two lessons, you'll learn how your choice of selection technique can affect the edits you make.

Time selections are related to the loop region that we discussed in Module 5, *Navigation and Zoom/View techniques*, Lesson 2, *Using loop playback mode*. You may have noticed that when you drag the loop region, a blue shaded area sometimes appears beneath the bar in the timeline. If you don't see the shading, double-click the loop region, and the shading appears. This shading indicates a time selection. Use the techniques you learned for adjusting and moving the loop region to adjust and move the time selection. To clear a time selection, click anywhere in the timeline.

When you make a time selection, any event that falls outside the selection remains unselected, and any event that falls within the selection becomes selected. What's not quite as obvious is what happens to events that fall partially within and partially outside of the selection. In this case, only the portion of the event that falls within the time selection is affected by the edit you make. Later in this module you'll see how a time selection that cuts through the middle of an event can affect your edits.

> *pt* **Private Tutor: Time selection shortcuts**
>
> A few shortcuts help you make exact time selections very quickly. For example, double-click the blank space between two events on the same track to make a time selection that covers the space between them. In the same way, double-click between the beginning of the project and an event to instantly select the time between these two points. Finally, double-click a blank area of the timeline (the dark gray portion where no tracks exist) or in the blank space just above the loop region to create a time selection that spans the entire project.

Task 8: Making a time selection

This task shows you how to make a time selection and adjust the position and length of the selection.

1. Open *M06Task007.veg* in the *LessonFiles\Module06* folder on the companion CD.
2. In the blank area above the time ruler, click a point between the two audio events in track 1 and drag to a point after the second of the two events.
3. Notice that the time selection fully includes the second audio event, and the event appears selected (as shown by the event's colored background). Notice that the first audio event is unaffected because it falls outside of the time selection you created in Step 2.
4. The second and third video events on track 2 fall partially within and partially outside the time selection. Notice that the portions of the events that fall within the time selection appear selected, and the portions outside of the selection remain unselected.
5. Click anywhere in the timeline to remove the time selection.
6. Double-click the loop region to restore the time selection.
7. Drag the loop region to the left and notice that this also moves the time selection. Notice that the left edge of the time selection follows the snapping rules that we discussed earlier.
8. Drag the yellow triangles at the ends of the loop region to adjust the length of the loop region and the time selection.
9. Keep this project open so you can use it in the next task.

Private Tutor: Remembering your time selections

pt

Vegas remembers your last five time selections and allows you to rotate through them so you can quickly restore them. To rotate through your last five time selections, press the **Backspace** key. Each time you press the **Backspace** key, you move one selection earlier. The sixth time you press the **Backspace** key, Vegas starts over with the last time selection you made and continues rotating through the last five selections again.

Now that you know how to select events and select time, you can easily make the third type of selection in the timeline: selecting time and events simultaneously. To make this type of selection, select one or more events using the techniques you learned in Lesson 1. Then, establish a time selection using the techniques you learned earlier in this lesson. In the next two lessons, you'll learn how this type of combination selection affects your edits.

When you use this type of selection, only events (or portions of events) that are both selected and fall within the time selection appear time selected. If an event is selected, but no selected event falls within the time selection, none of the events in the time selection are selected by the time selection.

Private Tutor: A quick combination selection

pt

To quickly make a time-and-event selection, double-click the event you want to select. This selects the event and establishes a time selection that matches the length of the event. If you then need to add more events to the selection, hold the **Ctrl** key while you click the desired events.

Task 9: Making a time and event selection

In this task, you'll become familiar with how the time-and-event selection affects the events on your timeline.

1. If the project you worked on in the previous task is no longer open, open *M06Task007.veg* in the *LessonFiles\Module06* folder on the companion CD.
2. In the blank area above the time ruler, click a point between the two audio events in track 1 and drag to a point after the second event. This is the same time selection you made in the previous task. Notice how the time selection affects each event that it touches.
3. Click the first audio event to select it. This also removes the time selection you created in the previous step.
4. Press the **Backspace** key to rotate back to the time selection you made in Step 2.
5. Notice that time selection no longer affect the events it touches. This is because an event is selected, but no selected events fall within the time selection.
6. Drag the loop region to the left until the beginning of the time selection rests near the midpoint of the first audio event (which should still be selected). Notice that the portion of the selected event that falls within the time selection has darker shading than the portion that falls outside of the time selection.

You now know how to make all three types of selections in the timeline. In the next two lessons, we'll explore how these different types of selections can affect the edits you make in your project.

Lesson 5: Cut/copy/paste/delete

Just like your favorite word processing application allows you to cut, copy, paste, and delete text, Vegas allows you to perform these operations on many of the items in your project. In this lesson, you'll learn how to cut, copy, paste, and delete events on the timeline. You'll also learn how the type of selection you make before you perform these operations affects the results of the edits.

> *pt* **Private Tutor: Understanding cut, copy, paste, and delete**
>
> Let's take a quick look at how these operations work. When you cut an object, you remove it from your project and place it on the clipboard. When you copy an object, it remains in your project and is added to the clipboard. When you paste an object, you add whatever is on the clipboard to your project. The clipboard can hold the results of only one cut or copy operation at a time. When you delete an object, you remove it from your project but do not place it on the clipboard. Therefore, you cannot paste a deleted object back into your project. Vegas uses all of the standard shortcuts for these operations: **Ctrl+X** for cut, **Ctrl+C** for copy, **Ctrl+V** for paste, and **Delete** for delete.

The simplest cases to understand are those in which you simply select an event and then perform a cut, delete, or copy. For instance, to cut an event from your project, first select the event. You now have several options. In addition to the keyboard shortcuts mentioned in the Private Tutor above, you can choose **Edit | Cut**, or right-click the event and choose **Cut** from the shortcut menu. Finally, you can click the **Cut** button. From this point on, we'll use only the keyboard shortcuts to accomplish the task, but remember that you can use any of the alternatives.

After you cut (or copy) an event, reposition the cursor and press **Ctrl+V** to paste the event at the cursor position. If you click in an audio track and paste a video event, Vegas creates a new video track to hold the pasted event.

Task 10: Cutting and pasting a single event

This task shows you how to cut an event and then paste it back into your project.

1. Open *M06Task008.veg* in the *LessonFiles\Module06* folder on the companion CD.
2. Select the first audio event in track 1.
3. Press **Ctrl+X** to cut the event from the project.
4. Click in the audio track at the last grid line before the remaining audio event on track 1.
5. Press **Ctrl+V** to paste the cut event back into your project. The end of the pasted event crossfades with the beginning of the second audio event where they overlap.
6. Keep this project open so you can continue working with it in the next task.

When you cut or copy multiple events and then paste them back into your project, Vegas preserves the spatial relationship between the events. For example, events that are on different tracks when you cut or copy them are pasted in on separate tracks. If there is a five-second gap between two events when you cut or copy them, there is a five-second gap between the pasted events too.

Task 11: Cutting and pasting multiple events

In this task, you'll discover the results of pasting multiple events into the timeline.

1. Open *M06Task009.veg* in the *LessonFiles\Module06* folder on the companion CD.
2. Select the first and third audio events and the first video event.
3. Press **Ctrl+C** to copy the three events.
4. Click to the right of the last event in track 1 to place the cursor there.
5. Press **Ctrl+V** to paste the copied events into your project. Close this project without saving your changes.

You can use a time selection to perform operations on several events across multiple tracks without having to select each event. When you make a time selection and then perform a cut, copy, or delete, only the events (or portions of events) included in the time selection are affected by the operation.

Task 12: Cutting a time selection

This task shows you the results of cutting using a time selection.

1. Open *M06Task008.veg* in the *LessonFiles\Module06* folder on the companion CD.
2. Make a time selection that extends from the middle of the first audio event to the middle of the first video event.
3. Press **Ctrl+X** to cut the time selection. Only the portions of each event that fall within the time selection are cut.
4. Close this project without saving your changes.

When you have a combination time-and-event selection, the results of a cut or delete operation become just a little more complicated. Let's talk first about the case in which you have at least one selected event and a time selection that contains all of the selected event. When you cut or delete the entire event is removed. Any events within the time selection but not selected are unaffected.

Task 13: Cutting selected events within a time selection

In this task, you'll cut a selected event that lies within a time selection.

1. Open *M06Task009.veg* in the *LessonFiles\Module06* folder on the companion CD.
2. Double-click the first video event in track 2 to select the event and create a time selection the same length as the event. Notice that the time selection also includes the second audio event. However, the audio event is not selected.
3. Press **Ctrl+X**. The selected video event is removed. Track 1 remains unaffected since no events were selected in that track.
4. Leave this project open so you can continue working with it in the next task.

If you have more than one selected event and only some of the selected events fall within the time selection, only the portion of a selected event that falls within the time range is affected.

Task 14: Cutting with selected events that fall both within and outside of a time selection

This task demonstrates how a time range affects selected events with a combination time-and-event selection.

1. Using the project you started in the previous task, select the first audio event and the remaining video event.
2. Create a time selection that starts over the space between the first and second audio events and ends at the middle of the video event.
3. Press **Ctrl+X**. The portion of the video event that fell within the time selection is removed. Notice that track 1 is not affected even though an event was selected (since it didn't fall within the time selection).
4. Close this project without saving your changes.

If the project contains selected events, but none of those events fall within the time selection, the cut or delete operation has no immediate effect.

Lesson 6: Ripple edit mode

You may have noticed that each time we cut, trimmed, or deleted an event—or portion of an event—in the tasks above, only the event was removed. The project time was unaffected and consequently all events to the right (later in time) stayed where they were. In some cases this is exactly what you want to happen. There are other times when you need to cut, trim, or delete an event *and* the time associated with it so that when you alter the event all the events later in time move to the left (earlier in time) to fill in the gap left by the altered event. This is known as a ripple edit. Vegas features post-edit rippling that you can apply manually or automatically.

When you make an edit, Vegas notes not only how the edit affects events, but also how the project time is affected, and adjusts the project accordingly. For instance, when you move an event so that it occurs later (or earlier) in the timeline and then apply a post-edit ripple, Vegas moves every event that occurs *after the start of the moved event in its original position* so that they maintain their relationship to the moved event.

Vegas offers three options for how you want the post-edit ripple to affect your project:

- **Affected Tracks** - Ripples only the tracks where you preformed the edit and includes events, keyframes, and envelopes.
- **Affected Tracks, Bus Tracks, Markers and Regions** – Ripples only the tracks where you preformed the edit and includes events, keyframes, envelopes, markers, regions, and associated bus tracks.
- **All Tracks Markers and Regions** – Ripples all tracks in the project and includes events, keyframes, envelopes, markers, regions, and associated bus tracks.

By default Vegas is set to manual ripple edit mode. You may have noticed that whenever you move an event in the timeline or edge trim an event, an arrow appears in the top portion of the marker bar as shown in **Figure 6.5**. This arrow indicates the direction and distance of the move. It also indicates the direction and distance that the project ripples if you choose to do so. To complete the ripple edit, choose **Edit | Post-Edit Ripple | Affected Tracks**. The first two events in track 1 ripple to the right the amount indicated by the ripple arrow as shown in **Figure 6.6**. The events in track 2 are unaffected.

Figure 6.5
The ripple arrow shows the distance and direction the event was moved
and the distance and direction the other events will ripple.

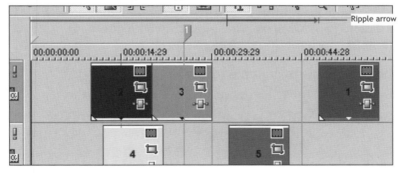

Figure 6.6
Choose **Edit | Post-Edit Ripple | Affected Tracks** to ripple the events in track 1.

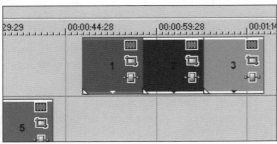

Task 15: Applying a simple ripple edit

In this task you'll move an event and then apply a ripple edit.

1. Open *M06Task010.veg* in the *LessonFiles\Module06* folder on the companion CD.
2. Drag event 1 to 00:00:44:28 on the same track. Notice the blue ripple arrow at the top of the timeline. The arrow starts at the point in the timeline at which event 1 originally started, and ends at the point in the timeline that the event now starts. This represents the amount of time that the other events will ripple.
3. Choose **Edit | Post-Edit Ripple | Affected Tracks**. Events 2 and 3 ripple to the right by the length of the ripple arrow so they maintain their original relationship to the moved event. Events 4, 5, and 6 do not move, nor does the project marker. When you choose Affected Tracks, you ripple only the events that are on the same track as the edited event.
4. Move event 1 back to the beginning of the project and press the **F** key. Events 2 and 3 ripple to the left to maintain their original relationship to event 1. You have just learned that the F key is the keyboard shortcut for **Edit | Post-Edit Ripple | Affected Tracks** and that ripple editing works in both directions.
5. Leave the project open for the next task.

Task 16: Applying ripple edits to multiple tracks

In this task you'll simultaneously move two events on different tracks and apply a ripple edit.

1. Using the project you started in the previous task, select event 1 in the first track. Hold the **Ctrl** key and click the event labeled 4 in the second track to add it to the selection.
2. Drag event 1 to the right again and drop it at 00:00:44:28. Notice that event 4 also moves since you selected it along with event 1.
3. Choose **Edit | Post-Edit Ripple | Affected Tracks** (or press **F**), and notice that this time not only do events 2 and 3 ripple, but so does event 5. Since moving event 1 also moved event 4, you had two affected tracks in your project, so the ripple edit was applied to both tracks. The edit does not affect the events in track 3 or the marker.
4. Close the project without saving your changes.

Task 17: Using ripple edit with the Delete command

In this task you'll delete an event and then apply a post-edit ripple that affects events and markers.

1. Open *M06Task010.veg* in the *LessonFiles\Module06* folder on the companion CD.
2. Click event 1 to select it and press the **Delete** key on your keyboard.

3. Choose **Edit | Post-Edit Ripple | Affected Tracks, Bus Tracks, Markers, and Region**s. Notice that this time the marker ripples along with event 2 and 3 since they are on the affected track.
4. Press the **Undo** button twice to undo all of the edits. Leave the project open for the next task.

Task 18: Using ripple edit with a trimmed event

In this task, you'll trim an event and then apply a post-edit ripple that affects all tracks.

1. Using the project from the previous task, point to the right edge of event 2 in track 1 and trim it so that it ends *after* event 3.
2. Choose **Edit | Post-Edit Ripple | All Tracks, Markers, and Region**s. This time all events in the project that start later than the edited event ripple, as does the marker.
3. Click the undo button until the original project settings are resorted. Leave the project open for the next task.

Task 19: Using ripple edit with the paste command

In this task you'll copy and paste an event into a different track and apply a post-edit ripple that affects all tracks.

1. Using the project form the previous task, right click on event 1 in track 1 and choose **Copy** from the shortcut menu.
2. Click in track 2 to place the cursor at about the 4-second mark. Right-click and choose **Paste** from the shortcut menu and select the **Create a new copy of source media** radio button in the **Paste Options** dialog.
3. Choose **Edit | Post-Edit Ripple | All Tracks, Markers, and Region**s. Events 2, 3, 4, 5, and 6 as well as the marker ripple to the right.
4. Close the project without saving your changes.

To significantly improve the speed of your editing, learn the keyboard shortcuts for the three post-ripple edit modes: Press **F** for Affected Tracks, **Ctrl + F** for Affected Tracks, Bus Tracks, Markers, and Regions, and **Ctrl + Shift + F** for All Tracks, Markers, and Regions.

To make editing even faster, use automatic post-ripple edits. Click the **Auto Ripple** button, as shown in **Figure 6.7**, to activate automatic mode. Click the arrow next to the **Auto Ripple** button and choose the desired mode from the menu shown in **Figure 6.8**. Now make an edit. As soon as you complete the edit, your project ripples automatically according to the mode you chose.

Figure 6.7
Click the **Auto Ripple** button to toggle between automatic and manual ripple mode.

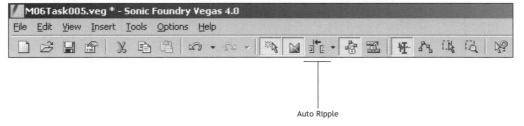

Auto Ripple

Figure 6.8
Click the arrow next to the **Auto Ripple** button to select one of the three modes.

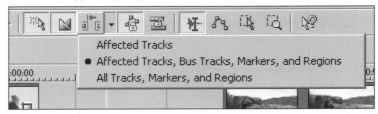

Task 20: Using Auto Ripple mode.

In this task you'll move and delete an event while in auto ripple mode.

1. Open *M06Task010.veg* in the *LessonFiles\Module06* folder on the companion CD.
2. Click the **Auto Ripple** button to select **Auto Ripple** mode.
3. Click the drop-down arrow next to the **Auto Ripple** button and notice that **Affected Tracks** is selected.
4. Move event 1 to 00:00:44:28. Notice that events 2 and 3 automatically ripple while the other events and marker remain unaffected.
5. Click the drop-down arrow next to the **Ripple Edit** button and choose **All Tracks, Markers and Regions**.
6. **Delete** event 6 in track 3. All events in all tracks and the marker ripple.
7. Close the project without saving your changes.

Task 21: Using ripple edits with a time selection.

You can use ripple edits with all of the techniques you learned above in regard to event and time selection. In this task you'll delete project time in ripple edit mode.

1. Open *M06Task011.veg* in the *LessonFiles\Module06* folder on the companion CD.
2. Make sure **Auto Ripple** is turned off and then double-click between events 4 and 5 in track 2 to select a time range.
3. Press **Delete,** and then choose **Edit | Post-Edit Ripple | Affected Tracks**. Since no events were selected, the time range affected all tracks, and all events on all the tracks rippled to fill in the deleted time range.
4. Click the **Undo** button twice.
5. Make a time selection that encompasses the middle third of event 6 on track 3. Notice that a portion of event 4 on track 2 is also in the time selection.
6. Press **Delete** and then **F** to ripple edit. Again, because no events were selected, the time range affected all tracks.
7. Click **Undo** twice.
8. Select event 6 in track 3 and double-click the loop region indicator to reselect the same time range as before.
9. Press **Delete** and then **F** to ripple edit. Only track 3 is affected.
10. Turn on **Auto Ripple** and select **All Tracks, Markers and Regions** from the drop-down list.
11. Double-click between the beginning of the project and event 6 to select the time at the beginning of the project.
12. Press **Delete**. Notice that all tracks and the marker ripple automatically to fill in the deleted time range.
13. Close the project without saving your changes.

Lesson 7: Splitting events

You'll often run into situations in which edge trimming isn't the best way to shorten an event. For example, it would be cumbersome to trim the right edge of an event that lasts for 20 minutes when all you want is the first 20 seconds. In such a case, splitting the event would be much faster. Splitting an event creates two events where once there was only one. In the example given here, you could split the event at the 20-second point and then delete the second of the two resulting events. In this lesson, you'll learn how to split an event or several events simultaneously. You'll also see how the selection type determines the results of the split function.

To split events, choose **Edit | Split** or press **S**. The results of the split operation depend upon the type of selection you made before executing the split. If no selection is made, a split occurs on every event that is touched by the cursor. If the cursor touches no events, the split command has no effect.

If one or more events are selected when you execute a split command, only the selected events that are touched by the cursor are split. Events that are not selected are not split, nor are selected events that are not touched by the cursor.

When you make a time selection without selecting any events, splits occur at both edges of the time selection in any events that cross the time selection edges. That means that if the beginning and end of the time selection touch a single event, the operation splits that event twice: once at the beginning of the time selection, and once at the end.

If you make a combination time-and-event selection, splits occur on every selected event touched by either edge of the time selection. Unselected events are not split, even if the time selection edges touch them.

Task 22: Splitting events

This task teaches you how to split events. You'll learn how the type of selection you make before splitting determines the results you experience.

1. Open *M06Task014.veg* in the *LessonFiles\Module06* folder on the companion CD.
2. Make sure **Auto Ripple** is turned off.
3. Click a blank area of the timeline just above the event on track 3 so the cursor runs through the middle of the event on track 3.
4. Choose **Edit | Split**. The event on track 3 and the audio event on track 4 are split.
5. Select the second of the two audio events in track 4 and press the **Delete** key to remove it from the project. This shows that the original audio event has been split into two and you can edit (in this case, delete) the two events independently.
6. Click the **Undo** button twice to undo the deletion and the split you made in Step 3
7. Click on the event in track 3 to select it.
8. Press **S**. This time, only the event on track 3 is split. The audio event on track 4 is unaffected because it was not selected.
9. Click a blank area of the timeline to deselect all events.
10. Make a time selection that starts in the middle of the first event in track 1 and ends in the middle of the second event in track 1.
11. Press **S**. Both of the events in track 1 are split because each touches one of the edges of the time selection. Notice that the second event in track 2 is not split because neither edge of the time selection touches it. Likewise, the events in track 3 are unaffected. The audio event in track 4 is split in two places since both edges of the time selection touch the event.
12. Press **Ctrl+Z** to undo the splits created in Step 10.
13. Select the two events in track 1.
14. Double-click the loop region or press the **Backspace** key until you reestablish the time selection you made in Step 9.
15. Press **S**. This splits the events in track 1 since they were both selected and touched by a time selection edge, but not the unselected audio event in track 4 (even though it was touched by the time selection edges, it was not selected).

Private Tutor: Keeping your splits straight

pt With all of these possibilities, how do you remember just how the split command is going to affect your project? You need to remember three simple rules. First, splits can only happen at the intersection of an event and the cursor or the edges of a time selection. Second, if no events are selected, every event touched by the cursor or time selection edges is split. Third, if any event in the project is selected, then only it and other selected events are split (if there is a selected event, unselected events are never split).

Lesson 8: Markers and regions

Markers and regions are valuable tools that help you in a number of ways. Among other things, they help you organize your project into sections, flag important points or edits on the timeline, assist you in navigating to various places in your project, and make it easy to quickly select portions of your project. You can add as many markers and regions to your project as you need. In this lesson, you'll learn how to use markers and regions.

> *pt* **Private Tutor: Using command markers**
> In this lesson we discuss regular markers and regions. In Module 8, *Delivering your project*, Lesson 2, *Rendering your project* you'll learn about another type of marker: command markers.

To place a marker in your project, move the cursor to the location in the timeline you want to mark. Choose **Insert | Marker** or press **M**. You can even do this while your project is playing. In fact, a common technique is to play your project and when you see or hear an important point, press **M** to place a marker without stopping playback. An orange marker appears in the timeline, as shown in **Figure 6.9**. The marker tab appears in the marker bar above the time ruler, and if **Snap to Markers** is turned on, the marker runs through all the tracks in your project.

Figure 6.9
Press M to place a marker at the current cursor position.

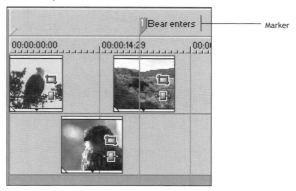

Notice that the marker tab contains a number to identify the marker (this is true for the first 10 markers you place in your project—the tenth marker is labeled "0"). These marker numbers help you to quickly navigate your cursor to the marker location. For instance, to jump directly to the location of marker 4, press **4** on your keyboard. Alternatively, click the marker tab.

If you place a marker when the project is not playing, a text box appears next to the marker. Type a descriptive label into the text field (such as "Bear enters" in **Figure 6.9**), and then press **Enter**. To change the label or add a label to a marker that doesn't have one, right-click the marker tab and choose **Rename** from the shortcut menu. You can also double-click to the right of the marker.

To move a marker, drag the marker tab to its new location. Moving a marker follows all of the snapping rules we talked about earlier. To delete a marker, right-click the marker tab and choose **Delete** from the shortcut menu.

Private Tutor: Deleting multiple markers

pt

Often you'll have several markers that you've used while editing a your project. When those edits are finished, the markers may no longer be needed. To quickly delete all your markers at once, right-click a blank area of the marker bar (the area that holds the marker tabs) and choose **Markers/Regions | Delete All** from the shortcut menu. To delete just some of your markers, make a time selection around the markers you want to remove, right-click the marker bar, and choose **Markers/Regions | Delete All in Selection** from the shortcut menu. Notice that this shortcut menu also gives you another alternative for inserting markers into your project.

Task 23: Using markers to organize your edits

In this task, you'll add a marker to your project, label it, and then use that marker to quickly align several events so that they all have exactly the same start time. When you're done aligning the events, you'll rename the marker.

1. Open *M06Task015.veg* in the *LessonFiles\Module06* folder on the companion CD.
2. Press **Ctrl+G** and type "22.23" into the **Cursor Position** box. Press **Enter** to move your cursor to that location.
3. Press **M** on your keyboard to add a marker at the current cursor position. In the box, type "Alignment position." Press **Enter** when you finish typing.
4. Click the audio event in track 1 to select it. Drag it to the right until its beginning snaps to the marker.
5. Drag all of the video events in the other tracks so that their beginnings also snap to the marker.
6. Double-click the marker label ("Alignment Position") and type in a new label, "Events Aligned." Press **Enter** when finished typing.
7. Keep this project open so that you can continue working on it in the next task.

In some respects, regions work much like the marker you added to your project in the previous task. For instance, they contain several common shortcut menu options, but there are some important differences, too. When you add a region to your project, you really add two markers simultaneously: one marker identifies the beginning of the region, and the other identifies the end of the region. You'll use regions to set apart various sections of your project. For instance, in a musical project, you might create a region for each verse, the chorus, and any other unique sections. In a video project, you might set a region over an important scene or video sequence. Once you've identified a region, you can quickly navigate back to it to work on it further. You can also copy the entire region (that is, all of the events within the region) and paste a copy of it to a new portion of your project. You'll find many other uses for regions as you work on your projects.

To add a region to your project, make a time selection of the area you want to identify, and then press **R** (or choose **Insert | Region**). Two green markers appear in your project, both of which contain the same number in the region tab. The first marker coincides with the beginning of the time selection, and the second with the end of the time selection. Double-click between the marker tabs to make a time selection over the entire region.

To change the length of the region, drag either of the markers to a new position. To move the region without changing its length, hold the **Alt** key while you drag one of the markers to a new position. To jump directly to the first maker, type the number of its marker tab. Notice that this also automatically creates a time selection over the entire region.

task

Task 24: Creating a region

This task shows you how to create a region and then use that region to make a copy of the events within the region that you'll then paste into a new portion of your project.

1. If the project you worked on in Task 15 is no longer open, repeat Task 15.
2. Right-click the tab for Marker 1 and choose **Delete** from the shortcut menu. (This step isn't completely necessary, but it helps to avoid confusion because you won't end up with a region and marker at the same spot in your project.)
3. Double-click the audio event in track 1 to establish a time selection.
4. Press **R** to make a region using the time selection. Name the region, "My first region." Press **Enter** to accept the name.
5. Click in a blank spot on the timeline to deselect all events.
6. Press **1** to move the cursor directly to the first marker of the region and create a time selection over the region.
7. Press **Ctrl+C** to copy the events within the region.
8. In track 1, click in a blank spot later in the timeline to place the cursor there.
9. Press **Ctrl+V** to paste the copied events into the project again.

pt Private Tutor: Undoing your edits

If you make an edit that you wish you hadn't made, Vegas lets you undo and redo edits an unlimited number of times. If you get far down the road, and begin to wish you could go back to where you were five edits ago, 50 edits ago, or 500 edits ago, just click the **Undo** button (or press **Ctrl+Z**) as many times as necessary to get back to where you want to be. You can also click the drop-down arrow next to the **Undo** button and choose the edits you want to undo from the **Undo History** list. If you decide you really liked those edits better after all, use the **Redo** button and drop-down list to get your edits back.

Conclusion

In this module, you've learned a lot of basic techniques for editing in Vegas. The techniques may be basic, but as you can see, they are powerful and allow you to assemble your projects quickly. You learned how to make simple and complex selections in your timeline, move events within the timeline, trim unwanted portions of your media, split events, cut/copy/paste/delete events, apply post-edit ripples, and add markers and regions to help you organize your work. In the next module you'll learn some of the more advanced editing techniques that make Vegas so powerful, but you already know enough to start creating compelling video and audio projects now.

Exercises

1. True or false: Vegas doesn't change the thumbnail within a selected video event because that would change the color of the clip in the final output of your video.

2. True or false: You can use common Windows selection techniques to select more than one event at a time.

3. Which of the following techniques allows you to change the state of the Selection Edit tool?

    a. Choose **Options | Define Selection Rectangle Size**.

    b. Hold the **Ctrl** key and use the left and right arrow keys on your keyboard.

    c. Hold the left mouse button down and click the right mouse button.

    d. Click continually on the **Selection Edit Tool** button.

4. Which of the following is not a snap point in the timeline?

    a. Grid lines.

    b. The midpoint of an event.

    c. The cursor.

    d. Project markers.

5. True or false: To temporarily override snapping, hold the **Shift** key while moving an event.

6. True or false: Before you edge trim an event, make sure to make a copy of the original media because the trimmed portion will be lost for good.

7. True or false: If your mouse has a wheel, you can emulate keyboard trimming commands with your mouse.

8. True or false: With the **Loop** switch for an event on, if you extend the event so that it is longer than the media it holds, Vegas repeats the media as many times as necessary to fill the entire event.

9. Which of the following is not a selection type in the Vegas timeline?

    a. Time selection.

    b. Event selection.

    c. Grid line selection.

    d. Time and event selection.

10. True or false: You can use event shuffling to quickly reorder the events in your project's timeline when roughing out an edit sequence or storyboarding.

11. Which of the following techniques lets you scroll through your previous five time selections?

    a. Press the **Backspace** key.

    b. Press the **S** key.

    c. Press **Ctrl+D.**

d. Triple-click the loop region.

12. Which of the following is the main difference between cutting an event and deleting it?

a. Cutting removes the event, but preserves the original media; deleting removes the event and the media.

b. Cutting leaves an empty event on the timeline, while deleting removes the event.

c. You can store three cuts on the clipboard, but only one delete.

d. Cutting stores the event on the clipboard, while deleting does not.

13. True or false: If two events are within a time selection and one of them is selected, the **Copy** command will place both of them on the clipboard.

14. Which of the following is not a valid post-edit ripple type?

a. All Tracks, Markers, and Regions.

b. Selected Tracks.

c. Affected Tracks.

d. Affected Tracks, Bus Tracks, Markers, and Regions.

15. Which of the following is not true when you press **S** on your keyboard?

a. If no events are selected and there is no time selection, every event in the project that is touched by the project cursor will be split.

b. If no events are selected and a time selection exists, all events touched by the edges of the time selection are split, and any event falling fully within the time selection is deleted.

c. If one event is selected and a time selection exists—but does not touch the selected event—nothing happens.

d. If a selected event is touched by both the beginning and end of a time selection, the event is split twice, resulting in three events.

16. True or false: You can combine markers and regions in the same project, but you are limited to a total of 10 markers and five regions.

17. Which of the following is not true about markers and or region markers (select all that apply)?

a. They are snap points.

b. Once established, their length cannot be changed.

c. They can be labeled with descriptive text.

d. They can be moved out of the way, but not deleted from your project.

18. Draw a line connecting the keyboard shortcut to the action it performs:

a. S   Paste

b. Ctrl+V   Select All

c. Ctrl+A   Insert Marker

d. M   Split

e. R   Insert Region

Essays

1. Describe a situation in which you would use markers in your project. Describe a situation where you would use regions in your project.

2. Describe the three rules that determine the behavior of the **Split** command.

3. Discuss the three different selections that you can make on the timeline and give example scenarios of when you would use each type of selection.

Module 7: Enhancing your project

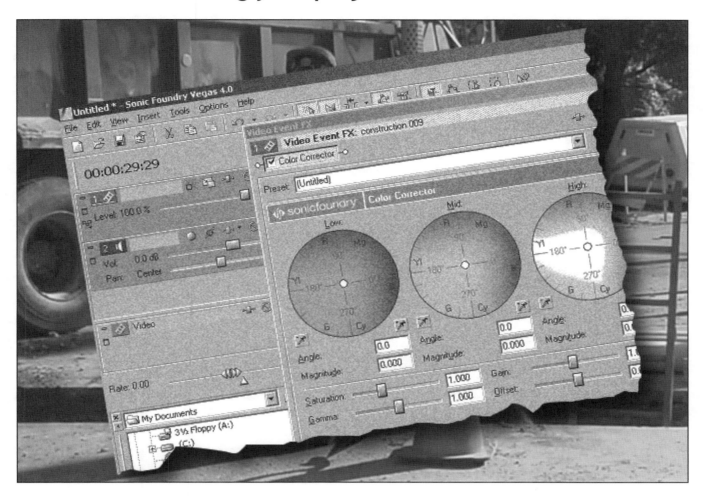

The techniques you learned in Module 6, *Basic editing techniques* helped you to begin assembling your Vegas project. Those techniques can take you a long way, but there's still a lot more you can do. The techniques in this module show you how to enhance your project to make it more interesting. After you've completed this module, you'll have enough knowledge to construct very sophisticated projects that include interesting special effects and advanced techniques.

In this module you'll learn how to do the following:

- Create fade-ins and fade-outs.
- Mix your audio tracks.
- Create fades with the master bus
- Put your movie clips into slow motion.
- Alter the look and sound of your media with filters and effects.
- Use the color correction tools
- Create sophisticated transitions between clips.
- Make multiple video clips visible at the same time.

Lesson 1: Creating fades

You've seen throughout the book that when you first add media to the timeline, Vegas creates an event to hold the media. The event has an abrupt beginning and end. A simple but interesting technique involves creating fades for the beginning and end of an event. This lesson shows you how to create audio and video fades.

Every event in your project has its own controls for creating fades. These controls, called the *ASR envelopes* for audio events, and *event envelopes* for video events, allow you to create a fade-in and a fade-out.

> ### pt Private Tutor: Controlling the sustain and opacity
>
> In this lesson, we talk about the "A" (attack) and "R" (release) portions of the ASR envelope. We'll talk about the "S" (which stands for "sustain") portion in Lesson 2 when we talk about mixing your audio and in Lesson 6 when we talk about video compositing techniques.

To create a fade-in, hover your mouse over the upper-left corner of the event. When your pointer changes to the **Fade In** icon (⟨⊿→⟩), drag to the right. As you drag, you create a slightly shaded area with a curved line running through it. The curved line represents the fade. The width of the shaded area represents the length of the fade.

You have several options for how the event fades into the project. To access these fade options, right-click inside the fade area. Choose **Fade Type** from the shortcut menu. A submenu presents you with thumbnails representing the following options, which are shown in **Figure 7.1**:

Figure 7.1
You have five fade-type options from which to choose.

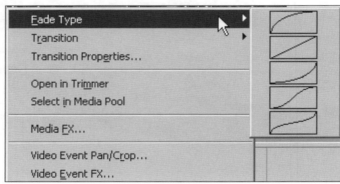

- **Fast**—the fade starts very quickly at the beginning and slows down at the end. (This is the default for audio events.)
- **Linear**—the fade takes place at a constant rate.
- **Slow**—the fade stars slowly and speeds up toward the end.
- **Smooth**—the fade starts slowly, speeds up toward the middle, and then slows down again. (This is the default fade type for video events.)
- **Sharp**—the fade starts quickly, slows down toward the middle, and then speeds up again.

To create a fade-out, hover your mouse to the top-right corner of the event. When your pointer changes to the **Fade Out** icon (←⊿⟩), drag your mouse to the left. As with a fade-in, you can change the shape of the fade. Right-click inside the fade out area and choose **Fade Type** from the shortcut menu. A submenu presents you with thumbnails representing fade types described above.

task

Task 1: Creating fades with ASR and event envelopes

In this task, you'll create a video in which the audio and video fade in and out together.

1. Open *M07Task001.veg* in the *LessonFiles\Module07* folder on the companion CD.
2. Click the beginning of the video event in track 1 to place the cursor there.
3. Drag the audio event in track 2 to the left until its left edge snaps to the cursor. The events in these two tracks now start at exactly the same time. Play the project and make note of how the video and audio start suddenly.
4. Click the end of the video event to place the cursor there.
5. Trim the right edge of the audio event in track 2 until it snaps to the cursor. Play the project and note how abruptly it ends.
6. Hover your mouse over the upper-left corner of the video event until you see the **Fade In** icon.
7. Drag to the right about one quarter of the way through the video event to create a fade-in.
8. Right-click inside the fade area, choose **Fade Type** from the shortcut menu, and then choose the **Slow Fade** icon from the submenu.
9. Create a slow fade out on the video event that lasts for about the last quarter of the event.
10. Play the project. The video fades nicely now, but the audio still starts and stops abruptly.
11. Click in the video event at the edge of the fade-in.
12. Create a slow fade-in on the audio event that matches the one on the video event. Drag the fade area until it snaps to the cursor.
13. Create a slow fade-out on the audio event that matches the one on the video event.
14. Play your project and notice how the video and audio fade in and out together.
15. Close this project without saving your changes.

pt **Private Tutor: Finding important locations in an event**

To quickly jump to the beginning and end of an event as well as the end of a fade-in and the beginning of a fade-out, click in the track that holds the event with which you are working and press **Ctrl+Alt+Left/Right Arrow**. The cursor jumps to the next important event location.

Sometimes you want a custom fade type. Track composite level (for video tracks) and track volume (for audio tracks) envelopes give you the flexibility to create the exact fade type that you want. To add one of these envelopes to a track, select the track and choose **Insert | Video Envelopes | Track Composite Level** or **Insert | Audio Envelopes | Volume**. Choose these options again to remove the envelope. Alternatively, right-click the track icon and choose **Insert/Remove Envelope | Composite Level** or **Insert/Remove Envelope | Volume** from the shortcut menu, as shown in **Figure 7.2** (you can also press **V** on your keyboard to add or remove a volume envelope).

Figure 7.2
Right-click a track icon, and choose **Insert | Remove Envelope** from the shortcut menu.

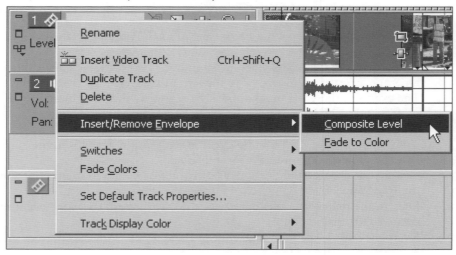

When you add a composite level envelope on a video track, a blue line appears at the top of the track. This line represents the envelope for the track. The volume envelope runs through the vertical center of an audio track. Because the techniques used for track envelopes are essentially the same for audio tracks as for video tracks, we'll use video tracks in our discussion.

Drag the envelope up or down within the track. With the envelope at the top of the track, the video appears completely opaque. With the envelope at the bottom of the track, the video appears completely transparent. Right-click the envelope line and choose **Add Point** from the shortcut menu (alternatively, double-click the line). Drag this point to another location in the track to create a fade between this point and the point at the beginning of the line (which Vegas puts there by default). Add as many points to the envelope as you want.

Right-click the envelope between two points and choose one of the fade types from the shortcut menu. Right-click a point on the line and choose a setting from the shortcut menu, or choose **Set To**, type a percentage into the text box, and press **Enter**. To delete a point, right-click the point and choose **Delete** from the shortcut menu. (You can't delete the first point on the line.) To return the envelope to its default state, right-click the envelope and choose **Reset All** from the shortcut menu.

Task 2: Creating fades with track envelopes

In this task, you'll create a video in which the audio and video fade in and out together. This time, however, you'll create custom track envelopes to do the job.

1. Follow the first five steps of Task 1, *Creating fades with ASR and event envelopes*.
2. Right-click the track icon for track 1 and choose **Insert/Remove Envelope | Composite Level** from the shortcut menu.
3. Drag the envelope to the bottom of the track. Play the project. You don't see video because you've made the track transparent.
4. At the beginning of the video event, right-click the composite level envelope and choose **Add Point** from the shortcut menu.
5. Double-click the envelope a quarter of the way through the video event to add another point.
6. Drag the point you added in Step 5 to the top of the track. This creates a curve from the second point to the third.
7. Add another point at the middle of the event.

8. Right-click the point you added in Step 7 and choose **Set To** from the shortcut menu. Type "50" in the box, and press **Enter**. This sets the composite level at that point to 50%.
9. Add another point about three quarters of the way through the event and set the composite level at this point to 100%.
10. Add another point at the end of the event and set its composite level to 0%.
11. Now create a similar volume envelope on the audio track, but use the following settings for the envelope points:
 -First and second points: -Inf
 -Third point: 0 dB
 -Fourth point: -12 dB
 -Fifth point: 0 dB
 -Sixth point: -Inf
12. Play the project to preview your new fade envelopes.
13. Close the project without saving your changes.

pt Private Tutor: Understanding the volume envelope settings

In the previous task, you set the audio envelope to specific settings, but why didn't we have you set some of the points to the very top of the track like you did with the video track, and what do those settings we had you enter for the points mean? You'll discover the answers to those questions in Lesson 2, which explores the basics of working with audio.

Creating a fade-out ending on one track is easy, but your project may have many tracks. If so, using track envelopes on every track could be a time-consuming and potentially inaccurate method of making the project fade out. You can use bus tracks to solve this problem.

Every project has two bus tracks by default: the video bus track, which controls the output of all video tracks in the project and the master bus track, which controls the output of all audio tracks in the project (as long as you have not rerouted any of the tracks to bypass the master bus). To view your project's bus tracks, choose **View | Audio Bus Tracks** and **View | Video Bus Track**. Bus tracks appear in a separate section at the bottom of the timeline. This section of the timeline has its own scroll bars so you can scroll to see other bus tracks if you have more than one. Drag the horizontal bar that separates bus tracks from regular tracks to resize the bus track area so you can see more than one bus track at once.

Notice that bus track headers contain many of the same controls as regular track headers, as well as some of the controls available in the buses themselves. Right-click a bus track header, and notice that you can add envelopes to bus tacks in the same manner as you do with individual tracks.

Task3: Creating fades with the Video and Master Bus

In this task you'll explore a way to create a fade on multiple audio tracks using the master bus and then match the audio fade to the video fade using the video bus.

1. Open *M07Task003.veg* in the *LessonFiles\Module07* folder on the companion CD.
2. **Play** the project and notice that both audio and video end abruptly.
3. Choose **View | Audio Bus Tracks and View | Video Bus Track**
4. Adjust your project layout so that you can see tracks 1 and 2 and the video bus and the master bus.
5. Right-click the track icon for the video bus and choose **Insert/Remove Envelope | Fade to Color**.
6. Right-click the track icon for the master bus and choose **Insert/Remove Envelope | Volume**.
7. Place a marker at 00:00:24:00 (place the cursor and press the **M** key to place a marker) and label it "fade start."
8. Place another marker at the end of the video and label it "fade end."

9. Double-click the envelope in the video bus track at the first marker to create a point. Create a point at the second marker as well.
10. Drag the second point all the way down to **100% Bottom Color**. This creates a video fade-out.
11. Place points at the first and second markers on the envelope for the master bus.
12. Drag the second point all the way down to **–inf. dB**. The audio now fades to match the video fade.
13. Play the project and experience the results of adding these envelopes.
14. Close the project without saving the changes.

Lesson 2: Basic audio mixing

Your Vegas projects will typically contain one or more audio tracks. When you add audio to your projects, Vegas gives you powerful tools to use in creating the perfect mix of all the audio elements. In this lesson, you'll learn the basics of creating a pleasant audio mix.

Vegas supplies several tools for use in creating the perfect audio mix. The most obvious tools are in the track header for each audio track. When you first add an audio track, the **Vol** fader (volume fader) rests at 0.0 dB. Drag the **Vol** fader to the right to increase the volume of the track or to the left to decrease the volume.

Private Tutor: Understanding volume

Volume is measured in a unit called *decibels* (abbreviated dB). A decibel level of 0.0 dB indicates the natural volume for the sound. In other words, when the **Vol** fader on a track is set to 0.0 dB, the volume of the audio on the track is neither raised nor lowered. A positive dB level indicates that the volume has been turned up. For every 6-dB increase in the volume setting, the audio is perceived to be twice as loud, so a setting of 6 dB sounds twice as loud as a setting of 0 dB. Vegas allows you to raise the volume of the audio on a track by 12 dB. Likewise, a negative dB level indicates a cut in volume. A setting of −6 dB indicates that the audio plays at half its normal volume. A setting of -Inf indicates no volume at all.

By default, when you play your project, the audio from each audio track is sent (or routed) to the Master fader in the Mixer window. From the Master, the audio is routed to your computer sound card and is then sent to your speakers. If you can't see the Mixer in the window docking area, choose **View | Mixer**.

The Master meter has a scale for each channel; left and right. Use the meter to monitor the overall volume of your project. A good target volume is a peak level (the loudest portion of the audio material) between −6 dB and −3 dB. The numbers above the volume meters (called peak indicators) show the highest volume, so play your project and watch these numbers. If they peak at too high a level, the audio is too loud, and you should decrease the volume. Use the **Vol** faders on the track headers to adjust the volume of individual tracks, or you can use the Master fader in the Mixer to adjust the volume of the entire mix. The numbers below the volume meters indicate the setting of the Master fader. By default, the Master fader rests at 0.0 dB so it neither boosts nor cuts the overall volume of the project.

Private Tutor: Clipping and resetting peak indicator values

When your audio is too loud, the peak indicator values in the Master meters may jump above the desired range of −6 dB to −3 dB. In extreme cases, they may go above 0.0 dB: this is known as clipping. Clipping causes unwanted noise and distortion in your mix. Remember, shoot for a value between −6 dB and −3 dB because that leaves you a little margin for error. For instance, if you set your volume so the audio peaks at 0.0 dB, louder audio later in the project may clip and cause distortion. If you leave a bit of headroom, unexpected increases in the volume will still likely peak beneath 0.0 dB. When the Master meters do peak at or above 0.0 dB, the peak numbers above the meters appear in a red box as a visual warning that your audio is too loud, and you should make the proper volume adjustments. After adjusting the volume, double-click the peak indicators to reset them so you can monitor your new peak values.

Private Tutor: Saving your project

pt

During the remainder of this module, you'll work on several tasks to build one project. We'll talk more about saving a project in the next module, but since the work you do in each task builds upon the previous task, you might want to save your work as you go along just in case you need to stop in the middle of this module. Use the standard Windows save techniques to save your Vegas project. The easiest method is to press **Ctrl+S**.

Task 4: Adjusting the volume of a track and the overall mix

This task shows you how to adjust the volume of an individual audio track and the volume of the entire mix.

1. Open *M07Task004.veg* in the *LessonFiles\Module07* folder on the companion CD. We'll work with this mock television promotional video through the next several tasks.
2. If the video and master bus tracks are still visible, use the View menu to close them.
3. Play the project. Watch the Master meter and note that the audio peaks well below the suggested peak range.
4. Drag the **Vol** fader on track 2 to the right to increase the volume of the audio on that track. As you do so, watch the Master meter, and stop increasing the volume when the meter peaks between –6 dB and –3 dB. (A setting of about 9.0 dB works.)
5. Double-click the **Vol** fader to reset it to 0.0 dB.
6. Play the project again, and this time use the **Master** fader to boost the audio until it peaks within the desired range.
7. Keep this project open so you can work on it in the next task.

Private Tutor: Setting your audio levels

pt

When adjusting the audio for your tracks, don't confuse the setting of the **Vol** fader with the peak level in the master bus. In Step 3 of the previous task, a setting of 9.0 dB for the **Vol** fader results in a peak level that falls within the desired –6.0 dB to –3.0 dB range in the Master volume meter. The peak level in the Master is the important thing to concentrate on. Set the track's **Vol** fader to whatever level achieves an acceptable peak in the Master.

Notice that the waveform for the audio event in track 2 of the project is very small. This indicates that the levels where not properly set when this file was recorded. To fix the problem, normalize the event. Normalization is a process by which Vegas raises the volume of the audio so that loudest point reaches a specified level. To normalize an event, select the event and choose **Edit | Switches | Normalize**. Alternatively, right-click the event and choose **Switches | Normalize** from the shortcut menu.

Task 5: Normalizing an event

In this task, you'll normalize an audio event and then adjust the volume levels to avoid clipping.

1. If the project you began in the previous task is no longer open, repeat Task 4, *Adjusting the volume of a track and the overall mix.*
2. Right-click the audio event in track 2, and choose **Switches | Normalize** from the shortcut menu. The waveform is now much more prominent within the event.
3. Play the project and watch the Master meter. You now have a clipping problem.
4. Double-click the Master fader to reset it to 0.0 dB. Play the project and notice that although the project no longer clips, the peaks are still too loud.
5. Adjust the **Vol** fader in the track header to decrease the volume until the peak level in the Master meter is acceptable. A setting of about -3.0 dB does the trick.
6. Keep this project open so you can work with it in the next task.

Private Tutor: Setting the normalization level

To specify a normalization level, choose **Options | Preferences**, select the **Audio** tab, and change the value in the **Normalize peak level (dB)** box.

Private Tutor: Using other switches

When you right-click an event and choose **Switches** from the shortcut menu, you notice several other switches in addition to **Normalize**. We discussed **Loop** in Module 6, *Basic editing techniques*, Lesson 4, *Edge trimming events*. You should also become familiar with two of the other switches. **Mute** removes the event's audio from the mix; although the muted event remains visible in the project, you can't hear it. **Lock** prevents you from inadvertently editing an event that you don't want to alter.

Another common problem in audio files occurs when one part of the file is louder than other parts. Although a quiet section of the audio will be made louder with normalization, it remains quiet in comparison to the louder portion of the audio. *Compression* has the effect of evening out the audio level of various portions of the audio file so that the quiet sections' peaks more closely match the louder sections. To apply compression to an audio track, click the **Track FX** button to open the **Audio Plug-In** window, shown in **Figure 7.3**. This window contains three track filters: **Track Noise Gate**, **Track EQ**, and **Track Compressor**. Click the **Track Compressor** button at the top of the window. Choose a preset from the **Preset** drop-down list or make manual adjustments to the controls.

Figure 7.3
The **Audio Plug-In** window with the Track Compression plug-in screen.

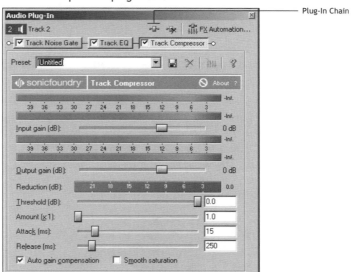

Task 6: Adding compression

This task shows you how to add compression to the narration so that the quiet portions' levels are closer to the loud portions, thus creating a more even narration.

1. If the project you worked on in the previous two tasks is no longer open, repeat Tasks 4 and 5.
2. Play the project and watch the Master meter as the narration plays. Notice that when the narrator says, "A young nation," the meter hovers around –9 dB. When he says, "a young country lawyer," the meter hovers around –15 dB.

3. Click the **Track FX** button to open the **Audio Plug-In** window. If the Audio Plug-In window obscures the Mixer window, move one or the other to a new location so that you can see them both.
4. Click the **Track Compressor** button.
5. Choose **3:1 compression starting at –15 dB** from the **Preset** drop-down list.
6. Play the project and notice that the two sections mentioned in Step 2 now generally hover around much more similar levels.
7. The compression increases the overall volume of the track slightly, so adjust the volume of the track accordingly. A setting of around –5 dB works well.
8. Click the **Close** button in the Audio Plug-In window.
9. Keep this project open so you can work on it in the next task.

Private Tutor: Using Vegas audio effects

pt

You can add many more audio effects to your track. Click the **Plug-In Chain** button (shown in **Figure 7.3**) to open the **Plug-In Chooser** window (we'll talk more about the Plug-In Chooser in Lesson 4). From there, you can add any of the available plug-ins to the chain. You can then adjust to achieve the sound or effect you want. You can also add audio filters and effects to the master bus if you want to apply them to the entire mix.

Since the output of each track is routed to the Mixer, you have two issues to consider in creating a final mix when your project contains more than one audio track. First, you need to make sure that the volume levels of the various audio tracks creates a pleasing mix (for example, the narration should be louder than the background music, or the drums shouldn't overpower the singer), and second, you must make sure that the combined audio output from all tracks does not cause the Mixer meters to peak at too high a level.

Two buttons on the audio track header help you create your mix. The **Mute** button temporarily removes the track from the mix so that you can concentrate on other tracks. The **Solo** button mutes every other track so that you can concentrate on the soloed track.

Sometimes simply setting the **Vol** fader on a track doesn't solve all of your problems. For instance, imagine a project that has a musical introduction. The music continues to play while a narrator begins to speak. Ideally, you want the music to be at a certain level during the introduction, but to quiet down (or duck) when the narrator begins to speak. Simply setting the **Vol** fader on the music track doesn't accomplish this. If it is loud enough for the intro, it might be too loud for the narrator to be heard. If it is quiet enough to hear the narrator, it might be too quiet during the introduction. In such a case, use the track volume envelopes you learned about in Lesson 1 to automate the mix (create a duck in the music track when the narration begins).

Task 7: Ducking an audio track

In this task, you'll add a music bed to another audio track, set the volume level for the music, and then use a track volume envelope to duck the music during the narration.

1. If the project you worked on in the previous three tasks is no longer open, repeat Tasks 3 through 6.
2. Add *SampleMedia\Audio\Abe'sTheme.mp3* to the beginning of a new track.
3. Normalize the event that holds the music.
4. Play the project and notice how the music overpowers the narrator. The music track also causes the Master meter to peak at too high a level.
5. Click the **Solo** button for track 3 so that you can only hear that track.
6. Play the project, watch the meter, and adjust the volume of the music track until it peaks at an acceptable level. A setting around -3.0 dB works.
7. Click the **Solo** button for track 3 again to bring the rest of the audio back into the mix.
8. Play the project. The mix is better, but the music should still be a little quieter when the narrator speaks.

9. With track 3 selected, press **V** on your keyboard to add a track volume envelope.
10. Add four points to the envelope on track 3 at these locations: 3.09, 3.29, 12.02, and 12.29. (Hint: press **Ctrl+G**, and type the numbers into the **Cursor Position** box to move the cursor to these locations.)
11. Drag the segment of the envelope between the second and third points you added in Step 10 until the value in the ToolTip reads -6 dB. This creates a duck in which the volume of the track is half as loud as non-ducked portions of the track.
12. Play the project, and notice that it is now easier to hear the narrator.
13. Keep this project open so that you can work on it in the next task.

Private Tutor: Controlling volume with track envelopes

pt

The default position for volume envelopes lies through the middle of the track instead of at the top. With 0.0 dB at the midpoint of the track height, envelopes allow you to boost or cut the volume depending upon whether you drag the envelope above or below the midpoint.

When the Master bus mode is set to stereo, Vegas can send audio along two channels (left and right) to your sound card (and thus out your speakers) to create a true stereo effect. In a stereo system, sometimes sound comes out of only the left speaker (hard left), and sometimes out of only the right (hard right). Sometimes sound goes equally to both speakers at the same time (straight up), giving the illusion that the sound comes from an invisible source between the speakers. Most of the time a sound is placed (panned) within the stereo field that runs from hard left to hard right so that it comes out of both speakers, although it may be louder in one speaker than the other. Controlling the panning of individual tracks and sounds is an important part of the mixing process.

Use the **Pan** slider in the audio track header, shown in **Figure 7.4**, to control the placement of the audio in the stereo field. Drag the **Pan** slider to the left to send the sound more to the left channel and less to the right. Drag to the right for the opposite effect. By default, the **Pan** slider rests at **Center** so the sound is sent equally to both channels. As you move the slider, a percentage replaces the word **Center** to indicate that you have moved a certain percentage of the audio from the opposite channel and added it to the channel toward which you are moving the slider. For example, a setting of "50% L" indicates that you have taken half of the volume away from the right channel and added it to the left channel.

Figure 7.4
Each audio track header contains both Vol and Pan controls.

Keep a close eye on the Master meters while you adjust the **Pan** slider. As you pan to one channel, your peak level for that channel increases (while the peak level for the other channel decreases), and you may run into clipping problems.

You can also control the panning on a track with a track pan envelope. Select the track to which you want to apply the envelope and choose **Insert | Audio Envelopes | Pan**. Alternately, right-click the track header and choose **Insert/Remove Envelope | Pan** (or press **P**). Pan envelopes are red. Add points to the envelope line and move segments of the line up to pan the audio left or down to pan the audio right.

Task 8: Panning audio

In this task, you'll add a couple of sound effects to your project and use a track pan envelope to distribute the sound effects in different locations within the stereo field.

1. If the project you worked on in the previous four tasks is no longer open, repeat Tasks 3 through 7.
2. Click toward the end of the music in track 2 to position the cursor there, and click the **Play** button. Press the **M** key to place markers as soon as you see the letter "e" appear in the Video Preview window. Place additional markers when the "d" and "u" appear, and when the word "television" first appears on the screen.
3. Add another marker a couple of seconds before marker number 1. This marker (marker 5) will make it easy to play the file back from a specific point in the timeline so you can view and hear the results of the work you'll complete in the next several tasks.
4. In all likelihood, you did not manage to place the markers in exactly the right positions. Navigate to marker 1. Hold the **Alt** key while you use your left and right arrow keys to move through your project one frame at a time until you find the exact frame where the "e" appears. Move the marker until it snaps to the cursor. Repeat the process to precisely place the other markers. You should now have markers in these positions: 16.08, 16.21, 17.04, and 18.06.
5. Drag *SampleMedia\Audio\Arcade Beep 05.pca* from the Explorer window to a blank area of the timeline to create a new track (track 4). Snap the event to marker 1.
6. Paste copies of the Arcade Beep 05 event at markers 2 and 3 (all on track 4).
7. Add *SampleMedia\Audio\Arcade Alarm 01.pca* to track 4 at marker 4.
8. Navigate to marker 5. Play the file and notice how the sound effects line up perfectly with the video. Notice also in the master bus meter that the peak levels for these effects are too high.
9. Adjust the volume of track 4 so that the peak levels are more acceptable. A setting of about −3.0 dB works well.
10. With track 4 selected, press the **P** key to add a track pan envelope.
11. Drag the pan envelope all the way to the top to pan the track hard left.
12. Add points to the pan envelope in the following positions: just before the first Arcade Beep 05 event, just after the third Arcade Beep 05 event, just before the Arcade Alarm 01 event, and just after the Arcade Alarm 01 event.
13. Drag the second point you added in Step 12 all the way down to pan the track hard right. Do the same for the last point on the line.
14. Navigate to marker 5. Play the project and notice how the sound effects move across the stereo field.
15. Notice also that the panning causes the master bus meter to clip. Adjust the volume of track 4 until the peaks are acceptable again. A setting around −8.0 dB solves the peak problem, but the sound effects are a little loud for a pleasant mix. Decrease the volume even more to achieve a better overall mix. Around −12.0 dB sounds nice.
16. Keep this project open so you can work on it in the next task.

pt **Private Tutor: Moving the cursor one frame at a time**

The right and left arrow keys move your cursor by one screen pixel. However, with **Quantize to Frames** active, the cursor snaps to the nearest frame boundary. Depending upon your zoom level, this could mean that a pixel on your screen contains several video frames. Hold the **Alt** key while you press the right or left arrow key to restrict your cursor movements to one frame at a time, even if that means the cursor moves less than one screen pixel.

pt Private Tutor: Control volume with the ASR envelope

In Lesson 1, you learned to use the event ASR envelope to create fades. You can use the "S" (sustain) portion of the envelope to decrease the volume of an audio event separately from all other events. To decrease the volume with the ASR envelope, hover your mouse over the top of the event. When the icon changes to a pointing finger/arrow combination, drag the sustain line down. A ToolTip indicates how much you are decreasing the volume.

pt Private Tutor: 5.1 surround mixing

If you really want to do some fancy mixing, set the **Master Bus Mode** on the **Audio** tab of the **Project Properties** dialog to **5.1 Surround**. This gives you enhanced panning controls that you use to place audio anywhere in the 5.1 surround space. Naturally, to take advantage of 5.1 surround mixing, you'll need a sound card and speaker setup that supports 5.1 surround audio.

Lesson 3: Creating slow/fast motion

Many video editors like to alter the speed at which certain clips play back to create slow- and fast-motion effects. In this lesson, you'll learn not only how to alter the speed of your video clips, but also how to adjust the playback rate of audio without changing pitch and how to change the pitch of your audio without changing the playback rate.

You can use a velocity envelope on a video event to speed up or slow down the playback. Velocity envelopes are applied directly to a video event (rather than to the track). Even so, the techniques you'll use to manipulate velocity envelopes are the same techniques that you already know from working with track volume, pan, and composite level envelopes.

To toggle the velocity envelope for an event on and off, select the event and choose **Insert | Video Envelopes | Event Velocity**. Alternatively, right-click the event and choose **Insert | Remove Velocity Envelope** from the shortcut menu. A blue envelope runs through the center of the event. This position is 100% velocity (normal speed). Raise the line to increase the velocity (speed the video up) by up to 300% (three times normal speed). Lower the line to create slow motion. Set the line at –50% to show the clip at half normal speed. Lower the line to 0% velocity to create a freeze frame. Lower the line past 0% into a negative percentage to show the video clip in reverse. You can lower the line to –100%, which plays the video at normal speed, but in reverse.

task Task 9: Slowing down a video clip with a velocity envelope

At the end of the video you created in the previous lesson, the word "television" zooms across the screen too fast to read. In this task, you'll create a velocity envelope to slow the video down at that point.

1. Open *M07Task009.veg* in the *LessonFiles\Module07* folder on the companion CD
2. Press **5** on your keyboard to navigate to marker 5.
3. Play the project and notice how difficult it is to read the word "television" as it zooms across the screen.
4. Right-click the video event in track 1 and choose **Insert | Remove Velocity Envelope** from the shortcut menu.
5. Add a new point to the velocity envelope where it intersects with marker 4.
6. Add another point to the velocity envelope to the right of the one you added in Step 5.
7. Drag the point you added in Step 6 down and to the left so it snaps to marker 4 (see **Figure 7.5**).

Figure 7.5
Align the two points so that the first is directly above the second.

8. Right-click the lower point and choose **Set To** from the shortcut menu. Type "50%" in the box to set the velocity at that point to half of normal speed.
9. Navigate to marker number 5 and play the project.
10. Keep this project open so you can work with it in the next task.

Task 10: Creating a freeze frame with a velocity envelope

The word "television" is a little easier to read at 50% of normal speed, but it is still difficult to focus on it. In this task, you'll modify the velocity envelope to create a freeze frame to give the viewer time to read the word.

1. If the project you worked on in the previous task is not open, repeat Task 9.
2. Hold the **Alt** key and use your arrow keys to move the cursor through the project until you find the point in the video where the word "television" is near the center of the screen.
3. Add a point to the envelope where it intersects with the cursor.
4. Add another point to the envelope to the right of the one you added in Step 3.
5. Drag the point you added in Step 4 down and to the left until it snaps to the cursor.
6. Set the velocity for the point you added in Step 4 to 0%.
7. Navigate to marker number 5 and play the project. Notice that the word "television" now stops on screen so you can read it. You might have to adjust the position of the two points you added in this task to freeze the video more toward the center of the screen.
8. Since you've frozen the video, it no longer fades out at the end. Use the event envelope for the video event to create a fade out.
9. Play the end of the video again to see your new ending.
10. Keep this project open so you can work with it in the next task.

Task 11: Creating reverse motion with a velocity envelope

In this task, you'll use the velocity envelope to play your video in reverse. You'll make the word "television" fly off the same side of the screen from which it flew on.

1. If the project you worked on in the previous task is not open, repeat Task 10.
2. Add a new point to the velocity envelope at the 19.20 position, and another one just to the right of that.
3. Drag the second point down and to the left until it is below the other point and its velocity is set to –100%.
4. Play the project to watch your new ending.
5. Keep this project open so you can work with it in the next task.

As an alternative to using a velocity envelope, alter the properties of an event to adjust the playback rate of the media the event holds. To do this, right-click the event and choose **Properties** from the shortcut menu. The Properties dialog opens with the Video Event tab active. By default, the **Playback rate** is set to 1.000, which indicates normal speed. Increase the value in the **Playback rate** box to speed the video up (up to 4 times normal speed), or decrease the value to slow the video down (down to .250, or one-quarter normal speed). When you've set the desired rate, click **OK** to close the Properties dialog and apply the new playback rate.

A jagged black line runs through the length of the event to indicate that you have changed the playback rate. Closer "jags" in the line indicate a faster playback rate. Since changing the playback rate does not change the length of the event, you may find that the media in the event finishes before the end of the event once you increase the playback rate. As you've seen in the past, the media loops to fill the entire event. Conversely, if you slow the playback rate too much, the event may end before the media has had a chance to finish. In this case, you may need to edge trim the event to see the entire clip.

Task 12: Changing event properties to alter the playback rate of an event

In this task, you'll remove the velocity envelope you've been working on and alter the properties of the video event to change the playback rate.

1. If the project you worked on in the previous task is not open, repeat Task 11.
2. Right-click the video event and choose **Insert | Remove Velocity Envelope** from the shortcut menu. Also, remove the fade that you created in the video event.
3. Since you want to increase the playback rate of the end of the video without affecting the rest of the media, split the event at marker number 4.
4. Right-click the second video event and choose **Properties** from the shortcut menu.
5. On the **Video Event** tab, change the value in the **Playback rate** box to "0.500" (half normal speed).
6. Click **OK**.
7. Navigate to marker number 5 and play the project. The results of this task are identical to the results you achieved in Task 8 where you used a velocity envelope to slow the video to 50% of normal speed.

pt Private Tutor: A shortcut for changing the playback rate

Vegas also offers a shortcut for changing the playback rate. Hover over the edge of the event as if you are going to edge trim it. Press the **Ctrl** key, and the mouse icon changes to ⟷. Continue to hold the **Ctrl** key and drag the edge of the event to a new position. The jagged line appears in the event to indicate that you have altered the playback rate. This method also changes the length of the event, so make sure that's what you really want to do before using the shortcut! This shortcut works for both video and audio.

Although you can't alter the playback speed of an audio event with a velocity envelope, you can change its playback rate in the Properties dialog just as you did for the video event in Task 11 (a feature known as *Rubber Audio*). Right-click an audio event and choose **Properties** from the shortcut menu. The Properties dialog opens with the **Audio Event** tab active. In the **Time stretch/pitch shift** section, choose one of the following methods from the **Method** drop-down list:

- **Change length, preserve pitch**—Speeds or slows the audio without affecting its pitch. For example, use this to make someone speak faster without making him or her sound like a chipmunk.
- **Change pitch, preserve length**—Changes the pitch of the audio without affecting its length. For example, you can adjust the pitch of audio that was played a bit flat in a piece of music without getting the audio out of tempo with the rest of the music.
- **Change length and pitch**—Changes the length and pitch of the media. For example, you might use this to create the voice of an alien who speaks very slowly and with a very low voice. This emulates the results of playing an analog tape faster or slower.

Depending upon which method you choose, you are presented with various settings to use in defining the playback rate and length of the media. Enter your desired values here and click **OK** to close the Properties dialog.

Task 13: Altering the playback rate of an audio event

In the previous task, you slowed the word "television" so it moved across the screen at half its normal speed. You now have a problem because the sound effect that goes with the movement of the word "television" doesn't last long enough. In this task, you'll change the playback rate of the audio event that holds the sound effect so the sound once again matches the video and change the pitch of a couple events.

1. If the project you worked on in the previous task is no longer open, repeat Task 12.
2. Place your cursor at the spot in the video where the word "television" has fully disappeared off the right edge of the screen (19.14).
3. Right-click the audio event in track 4 that holds the Arcade Alarm 01 file and choose **Properties** from the shortcut menu.
4. Choose **Change length, preserve pitch** from the **Method** drop-down list.
5. Click **OK**.
6. Hold the **Ctrl** key and drag the right edge of the Arcade Alarm 01 event to the right until it snaps to the cursor.
7. Navigate to marker number 5 and play the project. The sound effect now matches the video once again.
8. Right-click the second of the three Arcade Beep 05 events in track 4 and choose **Properties** from the shortcut menu.
9. Choose **Change pitch, preserve length** from the **Method** drop-down list. Enter a value of "3" in the **Semitones** box and click **OK**.
10. Repeat Steps 8 and 9 for the third Arcade Beep 05 event, but this time enter a value of "5" in the **Semitones** box.
11. Navigate to marker number 5 and play the project to hear the pitch changes you've made.

pt **Private Tutor: Changing length while preserving pitch: the fast way**

The default method for changing the playback rate of an audio event is **Change length, preserve pitch**. If that's the method you want to use, you need not go to the Properties dialog for the event to choose the method (as long as you have not previously changed it to one of the other methods for that event). Simply drag the edge of the event while holding **Ctrl** to change the playback rate, and Vegas applies the default method automatically.

pt **Private Tutor: Giving audio its due**

Don't ever let anyone convince you that you can skimp on the audio portion of your video. Audio has a huge effect in how your video is perceived. Prove it to yourself. Listen to the final result of all the work you've done over the last 10 tasks. Now, open *MO7Task004.veg* again. Play the project, and see—rather, hear—just where you started. Which version delivers the most punch? What's the difference? Aside from a few slow-motion tricks on the end of the video, the differences are all audio!

Lesson 4: Adding effects and filters

In Lesson 2, you added a compressor to the narration track to balance the audio level. As mentioned in that lesson, you can add many other effects (plug-ins) to your audio. Likewise, Vegas includes many plug-ins you can use to enhance the look of your project. This lesson shows you how to add video plug-ins and gives you a taste of some of the filters and effects included with Vegas.

To add a filter or effect to an event, click the **Event FX** button, shown in **Figure 7.6**. At the moment, the button is gray, indicating that no plug-ins have been added to the event. Alternatively, right-click the event and choose **Video Event FX** from the shortcut menu. Both of these methods open the **Video Event FX** window or the **Plug-In Chooser** window.

Figure 7.6
Each video event contains an **Event FX** button.

Event FX

The Plug-In Chooser lists all of the video filters and effects that were loaded on your computer when you installed Vegas so you can choose the ones you want to apply to the event. You can apply a chain of as many as 32 plug-ins to the same event. To add a plug-in to the chain, select the plug-in in the list, and then click the **Add** button (alternatively, double-click the plug-in in the list). A chain of buttons (one for each plug-in you add) appears across the top of the Plug-In Chooser. To remove a plug-in from the chain, select the button for that plug-in and click **Remove**. To change the order of the plug-ins in the chain, select the button of the plug-in you want to move, and then click the **Shift Plug-In Left/Right** buttons. When you're done adding plug-ins to the chain, click **OK**.

Task 14: Creating an effects chain for a video event

This task shows you how to create a chain of effects for a video event.

1. Open *M07Task014.veg* in the *LessonFiles\Module07* folder on the companion CD.
2. Click the **Event FX** button.
3. In the Plug-In Chooser, double-click **Sonic Foundry Black and White** to start a plug-in chain.
4. In the same way, add **Sonic Foundry Film Effects** and **Sonic Foundry Sepia** to the chain.
5. Click **OK**.
6. Keep this project open so you can work on it in the next task.

When you close the Plug-In Chooser, the Video Event FX window is displayed. The plug-in chain you created in the Plug-In Chooser appears at the top of the Video Event FX window. To change the order of the chain without going back to the Plug-In Chooser, drag the button you want to move to a new position in the chain. Click the **Plug-In Chain** button to reopen the Plug-In Chooser. To remove a plug-in from the chain from within the Video Event FX window, select the button for the plug-in you want to remove and then click the **Remove Selected Plug-In** button. Alternatively, right-click the button and choose **Remove** from the shortcut menu.

Each plug-in is initially added with neutral settings so it does not affect the video. To adjust a plug-in so it has an effect on the video, click the plug-in button in the plug-in chain. The parameter controls for that plug-in appear in the middle of the Video Event FX dialog. Choose a setting from the **Preset** drop-down list or adjust the controls to apply the plug-in to the video. To bypass a plug-in so that you can see what the project looks like without it, clear the check box next to the plug-in name in the chain.

task

Task 15: Adjusting plug-in parameter settings

In this task, you'll adjust the parameter settings of plug-ins to apply the effects to your video.

1. If the project you started in the previous task is no longer open, repeat Task 14.
2. Double-click the video event in the timeline to set the loop region over it. (You don't need to close the Video Event FX window, but you might need to move it out of the way. If you do close it, click the **Event FX** button on the event to reopen it. Notice that the **Event FX** button is now green, which indicates that a plug-in has been applied to this event and that the Plug-In Chooser does not open.) Press **Q** to turn on Loop Playback mode and play the project.
3. In the Video Event FX window, click the button in the chain for the Black and White plug-in. Choose **100% Black and White** from the **Preset** drop-down list. As you see in the Video Preview window, the video now appears black and white.
4. Click the **Film Effects** button in the Video Event FX window and choose the **Circa 1980** preset. This introduces video noise to the event to give it an old film look.
5. Click the **Sepia** button and drag the **Blending strength** slider to the right until the value in the box is ".400". This adds a greenish-yellow tint to the video.
6. Drag the **Black and White** button from the first position in the chain to the last position. Notice (in the Video Preview window) that the different order changes the video's appearance.
7. Clear the check box in the **Black and White** button to temporarily bypass the Black and White plug-in. Select it again to toggle the effect off and on to compare what the video looks like in color and black and white.
8. Close the Video Event FX window.
9. Keep this project open so you can work on it in the next task.

Use the keyframe controller at the bottom of the Video Event FX window to change the settings over time. Each plug-in in the chain has its own row in the keyframe controller, and each effect's keyframes can be adjusted independently. Revisit Module 4, *Adding media to your project: media generators*, Lesson 2, *Using the keyframe controller* for help with the keyframe controller.

The event is just one of four places in Vegas where you can add filters and effects. You can use the same techniques you just learned to add effects to the media clip (as opposed to the event as you did in the past few tasks), an entire track, and the whole project. Here's a summary of how adding filters and effects at these various locations affects your project:

- **Event effects**—Adds the plug-ins to a single event. No other event is affected by the plug-ins, even if other events contain the same piece of video media.
- **Media effects**—Adds the plug-ins to the media file. Applies the plug-in to the media itself: no matter where or how many times you use it in your project, the media contains the effect.
- **Track effects**—Adds the plug-in to the track. Applies the plug-in to the output of the track so that every piece of media used on the track appears affected.
- **Video output effects**—Applies the plug-in to the project at the final output so the entire video is affected.

task

Task 16: Alternatives for adding filters and effects

This task demonstrates how adding plug-ins at the four different locations affects the output of your project.

1. If the project that you started in the previous task is no longer open, repeat Task 15.
2. Right-click and drag *SampleMedia\Video\grizzlywalks.avi* from the Explorer window to the existing track in the timeline. Position it just after the event that's already in the project. When you release the mouse, choose **Video Only | Add Across Time**.
3. Adjust the loop region so that it spans both events. (The project should still be playing.) Notice that in the timeline, the two events look identical, except that the **Event FX** button in the first event is green to indicate that you have applied a plug-

in to it. However, you can easily see the difference between the two events in the Video Preview window.

4. Click the **Event FX** button in the first event. In the Video Event FX window, click the **Remove Selected Plug-In** button three times to remove all plug-ins from the chain. Now the two events are identical.

5. Open the Media Pool window.

6. In the Media Pool, you see a thumbnail for the bear clip (notice there's only one thumbnail, even though you've used the clip in two different events). If you had more clips in your project, you'd see a thumbnail here for each of them. Click the thumbnail to select it, and then click the **Media FX** button at the top of the Media Pool.

7. In the Plug-In Chooser, double-click **Sonic Foundry Spherize** to add it to the chain and click **OK**.

8. Choose **Maximum Sphere In** from the **Preset** drop-down list. Notice that now both events are affected by the plug-in (even if you move one of them to a different track) because you've added the plug-in at the media level.

9. Right-click the **Spherize** button in the plug-in chain and choose **Remove** from the shortcut menu.

10. Delete the second bear event.

11. Add *SampleMedia\Video\hawkMed.avi* and *SampleMedia\Video\eaglefly2.avi* (video only for both) to the space left by the event you deleted in Step 9. Adjust the loop region to cover all three events.

12. Click the **Track FX** button for the track that holds the three events.

13. In the Plug-In Chooser, add **Sonic Foundry Convolution Kernel** to the plug-in chain. Choose the **Bump** preset. The filter affects the output of the track.

14. Move the hawk clip from track 1 straight down to a new track. It is no longer affected by the track effect because it's no longer on track 1.

15. Delete the Sonic Foundry Convolution Kernel from the plug-in chain.

16. If the video bus track is not visible, choose **View | Video Bus Track**.

17. Click the **Video Output FX** button in the video bus track header.

18. Add the Sonic Foundry Light Rays plug-in to the chain and close the Plug-In Chooser.

19. Choose the **Intense Light Rays** preset. The effect is added to the final output of the project.

20. Close the project without saving your changes.

pt Private Tutor: Bypassing video plug-ins

To bypass any video plug-ins you've applied to the video bus track, click the **Bypass FX and Envelopes** button on the video bus track header. To bypass all video FX regardless of how they were added to your project, click the **Split Screen View** button in the Video Preview window to quickly see your project without effects and filters. The screen splits in half to show the video without effects on the left and with effects on the right. Drag a selection area across the Video Preview window to define the portion that shows the bypassed view, or choose one of the presets from the drop-down list associated with the **Split Screen View** button.

pt Private Tutor: Dealing with dropped frames

Filters and effects require extra computer processing power. If your computer can't keep up with the video, Vegas skips (or drops) frames. Every time a frame is dropped, the video looks a little less smooth. Click the **Quality** button at the top of the Video Preview window (if you've never changed it, it has the label **Preview Auto**). Choose **Draft Auto** from the menu. Vegas displays the video at a lower quality, which allows your computer to process more of the frames from the video so you can see smoother motion.

Another approach is to build a dynamic RAM preview that loads all of the frames within the loop region into your computer's RAM (or at least all that your RAM can hold). To build a dynamic RAM preview, define a loop region and then choose **Tools | Build Dynamic RAM Preview** (or press **Shift+B**). To allocate more RAM to this feature, choose **Options | Preferences** and click the **Video** tab. Increase the setting in the **Dynamic RAM Preview max (MB)** box. One more alternative is to temporarily bypass all of the video plug-ins in your project to decrease the processing demand on your computer. To do so, click the **Bypass FX and Envelopes** button in the track header of the Video bus.

pt Private Tutor: Copying event effects

You've just gone to a lot of trouble setting up various effects and switches on an event, and now you'd like to use the same setup on another event. To do so quickly, right-click the event with the settings you'd like to duplicate and choose **Copy**. Next, right-click the event to which you want to apply the same effects and choose **Paste Event Attributes**. This function copies event pitch shift, playback rate, undersample rate, effects, effects keyframes, pan/crop settings, velocity envelopes, and switch settings.

Lesson 5: Color correction

Vegas gives you great control over the color of your video with powerful color-correction tools that make highly accurate and professional color adjustments. When used in conjunction with the video scopes (see Private Tutor following this lesson), these color correction tools make working with colors in your videos easy yet powerful. This lesson looks at two of the color correction tools: *Sonic Foundry Color Corrector*, and *Sonic Foundry Color Corrector (Secondary)*.

Use the Video FX window or the *Event FX* button to apply the Sonic Foundry Color Corrector filter to an event. The Color Corrector filter, shown in **Figure 7.7**, contains three color wheels. The first wheel on the left adjusts the color for the low tones in your video (for example, shadows and other dark areas). The middle wheel adjusts the midtones (for example colors of medium brightness such as a neutral blue or green), and the wheel on the right adjusts the high tones (for example, areas of the video that are in bright light or contain bright colors such as yellow). On each wheel, adjust the white point at the center of the wheel to pick from a range of colors (the hue value) that runs counterclockwise from blue to magenta to red to yellow to green to cyan, and specify how much of that color (the saturation amount) you want to add to the affected tone range.

Figure 7.7
The Sonic Foundry Color Corrector filter gives you independent control over the low, mid, and high tones of your video.

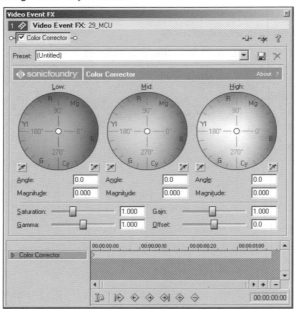

The angle at which you drag the color selector point determines the hue you add to the tone, and the point's distance from the center of the color wheel determines the saturation (or amount) of the color you add. The farther you drag the point from the center, the more saturated your video clip becomes with the hue toward which you drag. For example, to add more red to the midtones of your video, drag the point for the Mid color wheel toward the **R** just inside the edge of the color wheel (just over the 90-degree mark). As you drag the point, the values in the **Angle** box (which indicates the hue value) and the **Magnitude** box (which indicates the saturation value) update dynamically. You can also enter values directly into these text boxes to change hue and saturation. Double-click the point to reset the **Angle** and **Magnitude** values to 0.0 (that is, no color added).

Use the **Choose Complementary Color** eyedropper tool under each color wheel (refer to **Figure 7.8**) to sample a color from anywhere on your screen. Colors that appear exactly 180 degrees apart on the color wheel are complementary. For instance, yellow is the complementary color to blue, and red is complementary to cyan. When you use this tool to sample a color, the tool adds that color's complementary color to your video clip for the affected tone.

Figure 7.8
Use the eyedropper tools to sample a color from anywhere on the screen.

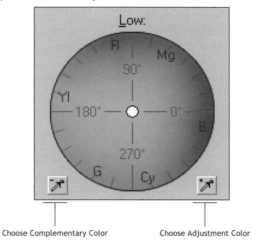

Choose Complementary Color   Choose Adjustment Color

Task 17: Applying a complementary color to your video

In this task you'll experiment with the **Choose Complementary Color** tool to see its effect on a solid color.

1. Start a new Vegas project
2. Open the Media Generators window, choose **Solid Color.** Drag the **Red** preset to the timeline, and click the event to place the cursor within it. Your Video Preview window now shows the red event.
3. Add the Color Corrector filter to the red event.
4. Click the **Choose Complementary Color** tool for the low tones, and click the red event in your timeline. This adds the maximum value of cyan to the low tones of your video clip, which has the affect of neutralizing the red to some extent. The red event now looks much darker.
5. Double-click the white color selector to reset it to its default position.
6. Close the project without saving your changes.

Click the **Choose Adjustment Color** eyedropper tool for the desired color wheel, and then click a color on your screen. This samples the color you clicked and adds it to the video clip.

The **Saturation** slider adjusts the video clip's overall saturation. Raising the saturation level creates more vibrant and intense colors. Lowering the saturation level essentially removes all color, giving you a black-and-white image.

The **Gamma** slider adjusts the overall brightness of the video. A higher setting brightens the video.

The **Gain** slider multiplies the luminance values by the gain setting. This has the general effect of lightening the video (raising the gain value) or darkening the video (lowering the gain value.)

The **Offset** slider enables you to set an offset value to be applied to all luminance values in the video. This provides another method of lightening or darkening the video.

Task 18: Exploring the other controls in the Color Corrector tool

This task will help you better understand high, medium and low tone colors.

1. Open *M07Task018.veg* in the *LessonFiles\Module07* folder on the companion CD.
2. Add the Color Correction filter to the event.
3. Using the Low color wheel, drag the color selector point in a circle around the outer edge of the wheel. Notice that this only affects the blue color bar in the event. The blue bar represents a low color tone.
4. Double-click the point to return it to the default position.
5. Repeat this experiment with the Mid and High color wheels. Notice that the Mid wheel only affects the green color bar (a midtone color) and the High wheel only affects the yellow color bar (a high tone color).
6. Close the project without saving your changes.

The Sonic Foundry Color Corrector (Secondary) Correction filter, shown in **Figure 7.9**, enables you to define a range of colors within your video to which you want to limit the color adjustments you make. With this tool, you can make very specific color adjustments to portions of the video without affecting other portions. Add the Sonic Foundry Color Corrector (Secondary) to an event in your project. Try to pick a video clip that has a large area of solid color such as a red car, a blue wall, or a green shirt.

Figure 7.9

The Sonic Foundry Color Corrector (Secondary) filter enables you to isolate specific portions of your video to pinpoint your color corrections.

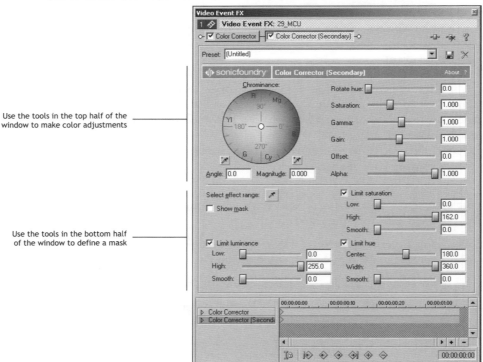

Using the Secondary Color Corrector is a two-step process. First, use the controls in the bottom half of the filter's interface to define the area of the video that you want to affect. Then, use the tools in the top half to make the desired color adjustments.

Let's break these two general steps into specifics. First, add the Secondary Color Correction filter to the event you want to work with. Click in the timeline to place the cursor within the event. As usual, the frame is displayed in the Video Preview window. Often, you can define the area you want to affect fairly closely with the **Define Effect Range** button. Click the button, then click and drag inside the Video Preview window over a portion of the area that you want to correct. For example, if you want to color correct a wall in the background of the video, click and drag over a portion of the wall without including anything other than the wall. You've just defined a mask, that is, the range of colors that the filter will act upon when you start making color adjustments. Select the **Show Mask** check box to see how accurately you've defined the desired area.

Usually, you'll notice that the area is not perfectly defined. You'll need to fine-tune it so that you affect only the object you want (in this case, the wall) and not other objects in the video that may share similar colors. First, you might try sampling different portions of the object. Try larger and smaller sample areas to see which gets you closest to a perfect mask. Then, make adjustments to the various controls in the **Limit Luminance**, **Limit Saturation**, and **Limit Hue** sections until you've isolated the object you want to color correct as completely as possible (it may not be possible to define the area perfectly, but experiment with different combinations of these controls, and you should be able to get very close in most cases.) There's an art to defining a good mask. The process requires a lot of experimentation, but with a little experience, you'll soon begin to learn what works and what doesn't.

Once you're satisfied that you've defined the mask as accurately as possible, clear the **Show Mask** check box. Now you're ready to make the color adjustments. The color wheel provides the easiest method for making color adjustments. You're already familiar with the color wheel from working with the 3-wheel Color Correction filter earlier. The color wheel in this filter works exactly the same way. Reposition the point to define the hue and luminosity of the color correction. Notice that the color changes affect only the area you defined with the mask.

The **Rotate Hue** slider changes the angle assigned to the colors on the color wheel. For instance, with this slider set to 180 degrees, each color on the wheel now occupies the position exactly opposite of its default position on the wheel, so that red now occupies the position formerly held by cyan.

Drag the **Saturation** slider to the right to make the colors more vibrant, or to the left to tone the colors down a bit. A very low saturation setting allows some of the original color to bleed through the color you're adding with the filter. This combination of the original color and the color-correction color can allow you to add just a touch of the new color to the object. A high saturation setting causes the corrected color to completely override the original color.

The **Offset**, **Gamma**, and **Gain**, sliders work as described for the Color Corrector filter. Adjust the **Alpha** slider to raise or lower the alpha value of the mask. The alpha value represents transparency. An alpha value of 1.000 makes the mask totally opaque, while a value of 0.000 creates a completely transparent mask. To see the effect of the alpha setting, place another video clip on a new track below the one to which you are applying color correction. As you lower the alpha value, you see the clip on the lower track begin to show through the mask.

Task 19: Using the Color Corrector (Secondary) filter

In this task you'll use the Color Corrector (Secondary) filter to adjust a single color.

1. Open *M07Task019.veg* in the *LessonFiles\Module07* folder on the companion CD.
2. Add the Color Corrector (Secondary) filter to the event.
3. Undock the Video Preview window and double-click its title bar to maximize the window.
4. Select the **Select effect range:** button in the Color Corrector (Secondary) filter and draw a rectangle that covers a large portion of the red shirt.
5. Select the **Show mask** check box. The area that can be color controlled is displayed in white. Everything else is black. Clear the **Show mask** check box.
6. Set the angle to 0.0 and keep the **Magnitude** setting between .400 and .500. Move the **Rotate hue** slider from far left to far right as the video loops. Notice that only the shirt, running shorts, and tennis shoes stripes change color because they are all the same color range. Everything else is unaffected.
7. Close the project without saving your changes.

Private Tutor: Other color-correction tools

pt Vegas offers more than these two color correction tools. Browse through the Video FX window for more tools to help you work with color in your Vegas projects.

Private Tutor: Video Scopes

pt When professionals are color correcting their images, they rely on scopes to accurately tune in the exact colors they're after. Vegas supplies four different scopes to help with the color correction task. Choose **View | Video Scopes** to open the Video Scopes window. Choose **All** from the drop-down list to see all four scopes at the same time. Click the **Update Scopes while Playing** button to see the scope information update as you play the video.

Lesson 6: Creating crossfades and other transitions

When you position two events on the timeline so that one begins as soon as the other ends, you've created a butt edit or cut. This is a very common editing technique, and you'll use it quite often. Sometimes, however, you'll want to have a more gradual switch from one event to the other, so that the first clip can be seen disappearing while the second appears. This is known as a transition. Vegas gives you many ways to control the look of your transitions. This lesson shows you how to create interesting transitions from one clip to the next.

The simplest—and arguably the most common—transition effect is known as a crossfade. In Lesson 1 you learned what fades are and how to create them. A crossfade transition is simply the combination of two simultaneous fades— one fade out and one fade in. Vegas has an Automatic Crossfades mode, which is active by default (to toggle Automatic Crossfades mode on and off, choose **Options | Automatic Crossfades**, or press **X**). To create a crossfade, add two events to the same track. Position the second event so that its beginning overlaps the end of the first event. The amount of the overlap between the two events (indicated by an "X") is the crossfade area.

In a crossfade, you can choose any of the five shapes (fast, slow, linear, smooth, and sharp) for both the fade out and the fade in, giving you 25 possible fade in/out combinations. Right-click in the crossfade area and choose **Fade Type** from the shortcut menu. A submenu appears with thumbnails of the possible in/out combinations. Choose a thumbnail to assign it to the crossfade (the default is smooth/smooth).

Task 20: Creating a crossfade transition

In this task, you'll create a crossfade between two events.

1. Open *M07Task020.veg* in the *LessonFiles\Module07* folder on the companion CD.
2. If Vegas is not still in Automatic Crossfades mode, press **X** on your keyboard.
3. Drag the second event (the eagle) to the left so it snaps to the end of the bear event (this is a cut edit). Create a loop region over the two clips, turn on Loop Playback mode, and play the project.
4. Drag the eagle event to the left so it overlaps the bear event. This creates a crossfade. Move the eagle event to the left or right until you like the length of the crossfade.
5. Right-click in the crossfade area and choose **Fade Type** from the shortcut menu. In the submenu, choose the slow/slow combination (the third thumbnail in the third column) and notice the subtle change in the crossfade.
6. Keep this project open so that you can work on it in the next task.

When it comes to transitions, crossfades are just the beginning. Vegas includes many different transitions. Each of those types has multiple presets and is fully customizable.

pt Private Tutor: Crossfading audio events

You can use the same technique you used in task 19 to crossfade two audio events.

To add a transition other than a crossfade, start out by creating a crossfade. Once you've positioned the two events, open the Transitions window (click its tab in the window docking area, or choose **View | Transitions**). The left side of the window lists the current transition types, and thumbnails for each available preset appear on the right side. Hover over any thumbnail to see an animated example of the transition. When you find the transition you like, drag the thumbnail from the Transitions window to the crossfade area between the two events.

The new transition replaces the crossfade as indicated by the blue or white horizontal bar that contains the name of the transition and a green "X". The Video Event FX window also opens. In the Video Event FX window, you can choose a different preset or customize the parameters of the transition manually. The keyframe controller at the bottom of the window once again allows you to create custom behavior for your transition. If you decide you don't like the transition you've chosen, drag a different transition to the area between the two events to replace the existing transition with the new one. If you close the Video Event FX window and then decide you want to customize the transition, click the green "X" in the transition area to reopen the window.

Private Tutor: Applying a transition effect to an event envelope fade

You can change the fade-in or -out that you create on a video event with any of the transitions available in Vegas. To do so, use the event envelope to create a fade. Drag a transition thumbnail into the fade area. Now instead of fading from or to black, the video transitions from or to black according to the transition effect you chose.

Task 21: Using transition plug-ins

In this task, you'll change the crossfade you created in Task 19 to a new transition type.

1. If the project that you started in the previous task is no longer open, repeat Task 20.
2. Click the **Transitions** tab at the bottom of the window docking area, or choose **View | Transitions** if the Transitions window is closed.
3. Select **Clock Wipe** in the list at the left side of the Transitions window.
4. Hover over the various thumbnails to see what your options are. Drag the **Clockwise, Soft Edge** thumbnail from the Transitions window to the crossfade area between the two events in the timeline. Close the Video Event FX window. If the project is not still playing, play it now in Loop Playback mode.
5. Select **Linear Wipe** in the transitions window to view the thumbnails for that type of transition.
6. Drag the **Left-Right, Hard Edge** thumbnail to the transition area to replace the clock wipe with this simple transition.
7. Add a new keyframe at the end of the keyframe controller of the Video Event FX window (which opened when you performed Step 6).
8. With the new keyframe selected, adjust the **Angle** slider until the value in the box to the right of it reads, "180" (or just enter "180" directly into the box). Increase the **Feather** value to "1.000." You've just customized the simple transition to create a sweeping/fading transition.

Private Tutor: Using discretion

Transitions are often overused by inexperienced video editors who fall into the trap of believing that they make the video look fancy, when in truth, transitions are very often just distracting. Cuts and simple crossfades are the most popular transitions for a reason: most of the time, they do the job best. In addition, over the years of movie making, certain transition types seem to have taken on their own implied meanings. Sometimes transitions can send a subliminal message about the video that is not exactly what you intended. Of course, other times, you can use that to your advantage!

Lesson 7: Video composites

A video composite occurs when you show two or more video clips on the screen at the same time. Vegas supports video composites in several ways, often times eliminating the need to use a different software application to create composites. This lesson provides a quick overview of the various techniques you can use to create composites.

Private Tutor: Creating composites with media generators

pt You've already created video composites whether you realized it or not. When you generated media in Module 4, *Adding media to your project: media generators*, some of the media had transparent backgrounds. The transparency of the generated media event's background allowed whatever was below your media track to show through (if there is no event below the transparent portion of the generated media event, the black background of Vegas shows through, so it may not *look* like a composite).

To create a composite, first add two video events to separate tracks and position them so one sits directly underneath the other. By default, when you view the video in the Video Preview window, you can only see the event you placed on the top video track (for example, assuming you have just two tracks in your project, you can only see the event on Track 1). To create a composite, drag the **Level** slider on the top track to the left. The lower the **Level** setting, the more transparent the track becomes, and the better you can see through to the next track below.

You can also use envelopes to create a composite. Drag the center portion of the event envelope on the top event down to make the event increasingly more transparent. You can also select the top track and choose **Insert | Video Envelopes | Track Composite Level** (or right-click the track header, and choose **Insert/Remove Envelope | Composite Level**). This action adds a track composite level envelope.

Task 22: Controlling track and event transparency to create video composites

This task shows you how to control the transparency of a track or an event to create composites of events on two tracks.

1. Open *M07Task022.veg* in the *LessonFiles\Module07* folder on the companion CD. Play the project in Loop Playback mode.
2. Drag the **Level** slider in track 1 to the left. Set the level to 60%. You can now see the clips on both tracks simultaneously.
3. Reset the level for track 1 to 100%.
4. Hover over the top edge of the bear clip, and when you see the pointer icon change, drag the center portion of the event down until you reach an opacity of 30%.
5. Reset the opacity of the event to 100%
6. Right-click the track icon for track 1 and choose **Insert/Remove Envelope | Composite Level** from the shortcut menu. The composite level envelope appears as a blue line at the top of the track.
7. Add a new point to the track composite level envelope near the center of the event and another at the end of the event.
8. Drag the center point on the envelope down to a composite level setting of 0%.
9. Close the project without saving your changes.

Some video filters also give you a means for creating composites. Any filter that causes a portion of the top event to be at least partially transparent creates a composite. Examples of filters in Vegas that fall into this category are Sonic Foundry Chroma Keyer, Sonic Foundry Cookie Cutter, Sonic Foundry Deform, and others.

Task 23: Creating composites using video filters

In this task, you'll use the Sonic Foundry Chroma Keyer filter to create a composite where the video in the lower track shows through a portion of the video in the upper track. By the way, this is one technique used by movie makers to put an actor somewhere other than where he or she was when the video was shot—for instance, putting the high-priced star on the edge of an active volcano.

1. Open *M07Task023.veg* in the *LessonFiles\Module07* folder on the companion CD. Make sure the project cursor is within the eagle event, but don't play the project at this point.
2. Click the **Event FX** button on the eagle event in track 1.
3. In the Plug-In Chooser, add Sonic Foundry Chroma Keyer to the plug-in chain and click **OK**.
4. In the Video Event FX window, clear the check box in the **Chroma Keyer** button to temporarily bypass the filter.
5. Click the **Pick Color From Screen** button.
6. In the Video Preview window, click the blue sky with the eyedropper tool. This selects that color as the transparent area through which the other events will show.
7. Select the check box in the **Chroma Keyer** button to engage the filter again.
8. Play the project and notice that the video clips in the event on track 2 now show through the sky portion of the eagle clip.
9. Raise the **Low threshold** setting to around "0.200" and the **High threshold** setting to around ".8000" to improve the effect.
10. Close the project without saving your changes.

You can also create a track that acts as a mask for another track. When you set up a masking track relationship between two tracks, the event on the top track acts much like a Halloween mask where the mask covers your face but has holes in it through which you can see your eyes and mouth. In the same way, the top track acts as a mask that covers most of the lower track, but has holes in it to let parts of the video clips on the lower track show through. The difference between a mask track and a Halloween mask is that the Halloween mask covers parts of the face so you can't see it, whereas the mask track makes the parts that fall outside of the holes transparent, so if there were a third track below the other two, you'd be able to see through to the third track. It'd be like you could see through your skin to your skull in the parts of the mask that don't have holes for the eyes. Now that'd be a scary Halloween mask!

To establish a masking relationship between two tracks, make sure the tracks are positioned next to each other in the track list (in other words, if the first track is track 1, the second must be track 2). Click the **Make Compositing Child** button, shown in **Figure 7.10** on the lower of the two tracks. This makes the top track the parent track that controls what you see from the child track (the lower of the two tracks.) Any white areas in the top track (the mask) allow you to see through to content from the lower track. Any black areas in the mask cause the content from the lower track to be transparent so you can see through to a third track in those areas.

Figure 7.10
Click the **Make Compositing Child** button to establish a masking relationship.

Make Compositing Child

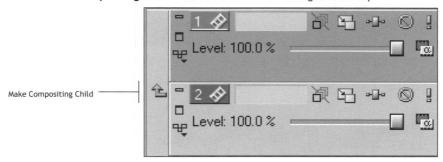

Task 24: Creating composites using a masking track

This task shows you how to use generated media as a mask to show portions of events in lower tracks.

1. Open *M07Task024.veg* in the *LessonFiles\Module07* folder on the companion CD. Play the project in Loop Playback mode.
2. Click the **Mute** button for track 2 to temporarily remove it from the video mix (you won't notice any difference in the Video Preview window yet).
3. Press **Ctrl+Shift+Q** to add a new video track at the top of your project.
4. Add the **Elliptical White to Black** media generator to the new track. Trim the generated media event so that it lasts for as long as the bear clip on track 2.
5. In the Control Points area of the Video Event FX window, click **Control Point 1** and enter "0.492" in the **Distance** box. Now both control points sit on the same spot, so there is a hard edge between the white and black portions of the media.
6. Close the Video Event FX window.
7. Click the **Make Compositing Child** button for track 2. The white part of the event in track 1 allows you to see through to the bear clip on track 2.
8. Click the **Mute** button in the track header for track 3 to let the media on that track show through where the black areas of the mask are.
9. In the event that holds the generated media in track 1, click the **Generated Media** button.
10. In the Video Event FX window, click **Control Point 1** and change the **Distance** setting to "0.266". Now there is a gradient in the generated media between the black and white. Notice how this makes a soft or feathered edge on the mask so that the bear clip fades out at the edges.
11. Close the project without saving your work.

pt Private Tutor: Creating a masking track

You can achieve some very interesting effects if you use another video clip as the mask instead of a black and white image. Try it!

With the **Track Motion** feature in Vegas, you can resize the video on a track so it no longer occupies the entire visible area of the Video Preview window. You can then position the smaller video anywhere in the Video Preview window. Any video clips on tracks underneath the track you resized show through in areas no longer covered by the smaller track, creating a picture-in-picture effect. Further, you can use the keyframe controller in the Track Motion window to add a shadow and a glow around the smaller track and set different keyframes to different positions to make the video fly around the screen.

To access the Track Motion window, click the **Track Motion** button in the track header of the track you want to work with (see **Figure 7.11**). Drag the handles of the position box at the right side of the Track Motion dialog to resize the box (see **Figure 7.12**). Drag outside of the position box (but within the dotted rotation circle) to rotate the box. Drag the box to a new location to move it. If you want to change the shape of the position box, first click the **Lock Aspect Ratio** button (the button is on by default, so you can't change the box shape until you click the button to turn it off). Next, drag the resize handles on the position box. When you change the shape of the box, you distort the video in the Video Preview window. Right-click the position box and choose **Restore** to reset the box to its original shape, size, and position. Select the **Shadow** and **Glow** check boxes in the keyframe controller to add these effects to the track.

Figure 7.11
Each Video track has a **Track Motion** button.

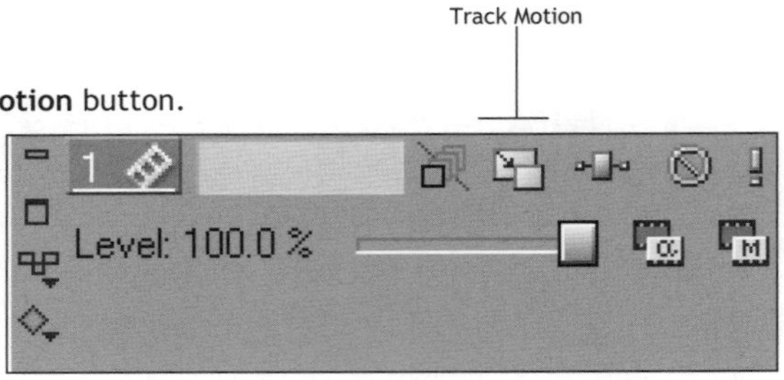

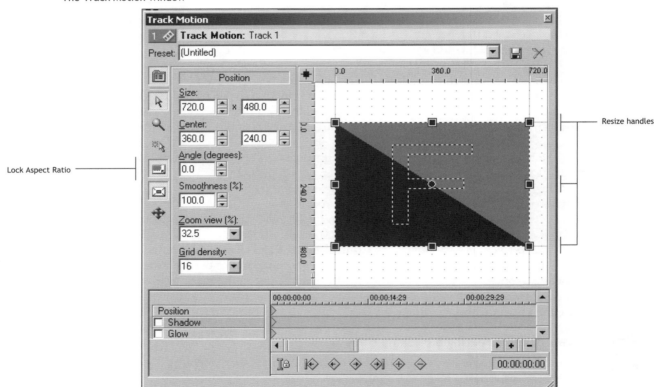

Figure 7.12
The Track Motion window

Task 25: Creating composites using track motion

In this task, you'll change the size of the top track to create a picture-in-picture composite. You'll also use the keyframe timeline to move the inset picture across the screen.

1. Open *M07Task025.veg* in the *LessonFiles\Module07* folder on the companion CD. Play the project in Loop Playback mode.
2. Click the **Track Motion** button for track 1. In the Track Motion window, drag the lower-right resizing handle up and to the left until the position box is about one-fourth its normal size.
3. Click inside the position box and drag the box to up and to the left until there is just a bit of space between the box and the edge of the gray area (which represents the area visible in the Video Preview window).
4. Select the **Shadow** check box in the keyframe controller to add a shadow to the track.
5. With the Shadow keyframe timeline selected (as indicated by the blue shading), drag the shadow down and to the right to move it farther away from the video.
6. Click the word "Position" in the keyframe controller to select the Position keyframe timeline.
7. In the project timeline, click the right edge of the bear event to place the cursor there.
8. In the keyframe controller of the Track Motion window, click the **Sync Cursor** button. This locks the cursor in the keyframe controller to the project cursor so that when you reposition the project cursor, the keyframe timeline cursor automatically updates.
9. Move the position box to the lower-right corner of the visible area.
10. Select the Shadow keyframe timeline. Drag the shadow to the upper-right corner. Notice that the track moves independently of its shadow.
11. Close the project without saving changes.

pt Private Tutor: Creating a split-screen effect

You could use track motion on several tracks to split the screen up into many small sections so that you can show multiple video clips simultaneously. This technique is a popular way to show the same scene from multiple angles or to show what several actors in different locations are doing at the same time.

You can also create a video composite with the Pan/Crop feature in Vegas. Since this is just one of the uses of this feature, we'll discuss Pan/Crop in the next lesson.

Lesson 7: Using the Pan/Crop tool

In addition to creating video composites, the Pan/Crop tool can emulate camera motion (such as panning and zooming) and crop out unwanted portions of your video clip. This lesson discusses how to use the Pan/Crop feature.

Pan/Crop is an event-level technique, which means each event in your project can be treated individually. To access Pan/Crop for an event, select the event and click the **Event Pan/Crop** button, shown in **Figure 7.13** (you may have to zoom in on very narrow events to see the button). Alternatively, right-click the event and choose **Video Event Pan/Crop** from the shortcut menu. The controls in the Event Pan/Crop window look and function much like those in the Track Motion window, but they achieve different results.

Figure 7.13
Each video event contains an **Event Pan/Crop** button.

Event Pan/Crop

Drag one of the resize handles toward the center point. This has the effect of zooming in. Click within the position box and drag it to a new location to zoom in on another area of the video. Drag outside the reposition box (but still within the dotted rotation circle) to rotate the video. Click the **Lock Aspect Ratio** button to lock or unlock the aspect ratio of your media. With **Lock Aspect Ratio** off, you can change the shape of the position box.

Look at the Source section just above the keyframe controller (you may have to make the Event Pan/Crop window larger to see the controls in this section). The controls here affect how the media within the event react to the changes you make to the position box. When selected, the **Maintain aspect ratio** check box prevents the source media from distorting when you change the aspect ratio of the position box. The **Stretch to fill frame** check box (when active) forces the source media to stretch until its dimensions (width or height) reach the edge of the video frame.

task Task 26: Using Pan/Crop to create motion on a still image.

This task shows you how to add interest to the still images you use in your video projects. In it you'll use the Pan/Crop feature to zoom in on a picture, then scan across the picture.

1. Open *M07Task026.veg* in the *LessonFiles\Module07* folder on the companion CD. Play the project in Loop Playback mode.
2. Click the **Event Pan/Crop** button on the event.
3. Drag the bottom-center resize point up until the top of the position box touches the top of the building. Since the **Lock Aspect Ratio** button is on, the box gets narrower as you make it shorter.
4. Drag the position box to the right until the edge of the box touches the edge of the building.
5. Click the midpoint of the keyframe timeline, and then drag the position box to the left until the left edge of the position box touches the edge of the building. Look at the Video Preview window. You've now emulated a camera move that pans across the front of the building.
6. Click the end of the keyframe timeline, right-click the position box, and then choose **Restore** from the shortcut menu. Now you've emulated a zoom-out camera move.
7. Close this project without saving your changes.

Task 27: Using Pan/Crop to crop unwanted material out of a still image

In this task, you'll repeat the first couple of steps of the last task with a slight change to see how different settings allow you to create cropping.

1. Open *M07Task027.veg* in the *LessonFiles\Module07* folder on the companion CD. Play the project in Loop Playback mode.
2. Click the **Event Pan/Crop** button on the event in track 1.
3. Click the **Lock Aspect Ratio** button to turn it off.
4. Drag the bottom-center resize point on the position box up until the top of the position box touches the top of the building. Notice that this time you do not change the width of the box. This has the effect of cropping out the material at the top and bottom of the picture. This creates a video composite that lets you see through (in the Video Preview window) to the Fireweed clip on track 2.
5. Clear the **Maintain aspect ratio** check box in the Source section. Since the picture is no longer bound by the rules of maintaining the proper aspect ratio (and since the **Stretch to fill frame** box is still selected), the height is stretched so that it fills the entire video frame.
6. Right-click the position box and choose **Restore** from the shortcut menu.
7. Select the **Maintain aspect ratio** check box.
8. Click the **Size About Center** button to turn it off.
9. Clear the **Stretch to fill frame** check box.
10. Drag the bottom center point up again. Disengaging **Size About Center** has enabled you to crop just the bottom of the picture.

pt
Private Tutor: Keeping it all straight

The controls in the Pan/Crop window can be confusing. Try to remember that the check boxes in the Source section determine how the source media is treated in reaction to the changes you make to the position box. Take some time to experiment with all of the different combinations of the source options to see what happens in different scenarios.

Conclusion

In this module, you've learned many advanced techniques you can use to enhance your Vegas projects. You know how to add several different types of envelopes to your project, and you learned how to create fades, crossfades, and other transitions. You also became familiar with some of the crucial aspects of working with audio that will help you create pleasing audio mixes for your projects. You can create video composites using a number of sophisticated techniques such as track motion, pan/crop, and track masking, among others. In the next module, you'll learn how to save your project and deliver your video or audio project for the world to see and hear.

Exercises

1. True or false: To fade the video out you must use a track composite level envelope; to fade the audio out, you must use the ASR envelope.

2. Which of the following is a valid fade type for ASR and track envelopes?

    a. Saw Tooth

    b. Square

    c. Smooth

    d. Sine

3. How many points can you add to a track envelope?

    a. 10 for audio; 25 for video.

    b. It depends upon the length of the event on the track.

    c. 10.

    d. As many as you want.

4. When mixing your audio tracks, which of the following is an acceptable target for your peak meter levels in the Master?

    a. −Inf.

    b. Between −Inf and 0.0 dB.

    c. Between −6.0 dB and −3.0 dB.

    d. Between 6.0 dB and 3.0 dB.

5. True or false: The term *clipping* refers to an audio level that peaks above 0.0 dB in the Master meters and can cause unwanted audio distortion.

6. True or false: To normalize an event means to automatically readjust the length of the event to match the exact, or "normal" length of the media within the event.

7. Which of the following best describes an audio "duck"?

    a. When you set the volume of a track to a level below 0.0 dB.

    b. When you set up track pan envelopes on two separate tracks to create an effect where when one track is sent to the left channel, the other track jumps, or "ducks" to the right channel.

    c. The use of a track volume envelope to gradually decrease the volume of a track over a given period of time.

    d. The use of a track volume envelope to temporarily decrease the volume of the audio on one track so that the audio on another track can be better heard.

8. True or false: When you pan a track more to one channel than the other, you should keep an eye on the Master meters because extra signal being sent to the one channel might cause the signal on that channel to peak at too high a level.

9. True or false: To create reverse motion, you can use either an event velocity envelope set to a negative velocity or alter the event's properties so that the playback rate is set to a negative number.

10. Which of the following is not a valid method for adjusting the playback rate of an audio event?

    a. Change length, reverse pitch.

    b. Change length and pitch.

    c. Change length, preserve pitch .

    d. Change pitch, preserve length.

11. At which level should you apply a video filter if you want the filter to affect every event that holds a specific piece of media, regardless of where those events fall within the project?

    a. Video Output Effects

    b. Event Effects

    c. Media Effects

    d. Track Effects

12. True or false: You can build a dynamic RAM preview to help your computer show a section of your project without dropping frames.

13. How many plug-ins can you add to each plug-in chain?

    a. 3

    b. 32

    c. 26

    d. 5

14. True or false: To create an automatic crossfade, you must set Vegas to Automatic Crossfades mode, add both events to the same track, and then overlap them.

15. True or false: Each of the transition types in Vegas can be fully customized to create custom transitions.

16. When you adjust the **Angle** parameter in the Sonic Foundry Color Corrector filter you are adjusting the:

    a. Direction of the light

    b. Amount of Color Saturation

    c. Hue

    d. Intensity

17. When you choose a color using the Complementary Color eyedropper tool in the Color Correction filter Vegas adds a color that is:

    a. 90 degrees apart on the color wheel

    b. 50 % brighter than the original

    c. 180 degrees apart on the color wheel

    d. 50% darker than the original

18. To make very specific color adjustments to portions of the video without effecting other portions, the best tool to use is:

    a. Color Corrector (Secondary)

    b. Brightness and Contrast

    c. Saturation Adjust

    d. HLS Adjust

19. Which of the following techniques cannot be used to create a video composite?

    a. Track Motion.

    b. Event Pan/Crop.

    c. Event Diversion.

    d. Masking.

20. True or false: If you change the aspect ratio of the position box in the Track Motion window, you distort the video in the Video Preview window.

21. Which of the techniques listed below allow you to create camera moves that were not really shot when the video was shot, or create motion on still images?

    a. Track Motion.

    b. Event Pan/Crop.

    c. Track Pan Envelopes.

    d. The Photo-Realistic Motion Generator Filter.

22. True or false: In the Pan/Crop window, the options in the Source section control how the video output reacts to changes you make to the shape and position of the position box.

23. Draw a line connecting the keyboard shortcut to the action it performs

a. Ctrl+Alt+Left/Right arrow	Insert/Remove Track Volume envelope
b. V	Insert/Remove Track Pan envelope
c. P	Build Dynamic RAM Preview
d. Shift+B	Toggle Automatic Crossfades on and off
e. X	Move cursor to the next important point in an event

Essays

1. Pick two of the video compositing techniques that we discussed in this module and describe how they are commonly used on the local nightly news.st

2. Discuss a situation in which it makes sense to use ASR and event envelopes to create a fade out, and contrast that to a situation in which it makes more sense to use track composite level (for video tracks) and track volume (for audio tracks) envelopes.

3. We suggested in this module that the heavy use of transitions could be distracting. Still, there are times when a special transition effect is just the perfect way to get from one video clip to another. Describe a scenario in which a fancy transition is more appropriate than a jump cut or simple crossfade.

Module 8: Delivering your project

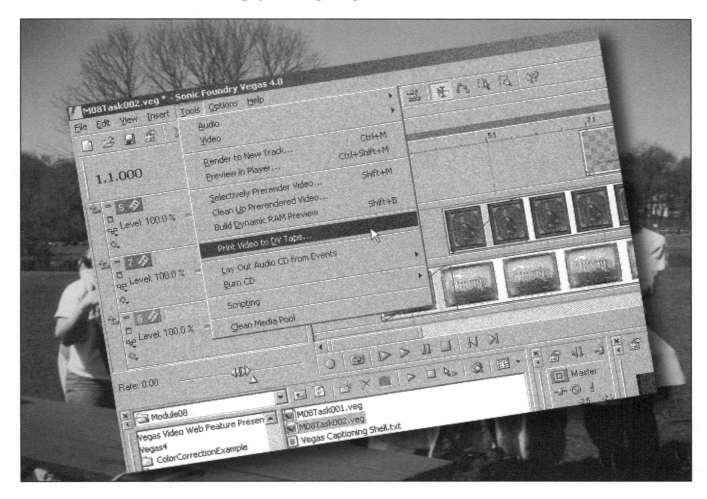

We've come a long way, and now it's time to share your Vegas creations with the world. This module shows you how to save your projects and deliver them to your audience. Whether you want to make your videos available on CD, print them to video tape, or post them to your Web site so that anyone can view them on demand, Vegas can help you deliver.

In this module you'll learn how to do the following:

- Save your Vegas project.
- Save trimmed copies of the media clips used in your project.
- Render your project into formats that other computers can play.
- Prepare your project for delivery via the Internet.
- Print your video project to DV tape using Sonic Foundry Video Capture.
- Print your project to DV tape from the timeline.

Lesson 1: Saving your project

Of course, as with any other software application, it's important that you get into the habit of saving your work early and often when you're working on your Vegas projects. In this module, we'll explore issues related to saving your work. In many other applications (such as a word processing application, for instance), what you save is essentially what you show your audience. In contrast, your audience probably never sees your Vegas project files. When you save your Vegas projects, you save all the elements that go into making your video or audio project. To create the final product that you'll present to your audience, you'll render your project, and possibly print it to tape. Rendering and print-to-tape issues are covered in the other two lessons in this module. For now, let's concentrate on saving your work so you can come back to it later and work on it further.

The commands you use to save your Vegas projects are no different than those you use to save your work in most other Windows software programs. You have all of the traditional options:

- Choose **File | Save**.
- Choose **File | Save As**.
- Click the **Save** button in the Vegas toolbar.
- Press **Ctrl+S**.

The first time you save your project (regardless of which method you use), Vegas opens the Save As dialog. As with most other programs, after you've saved your project for the first time, subsequent saves do not open the Save As dialog unless you use the **File | Save As** command.

> ### *pt* Private Tutor: Saving often
>
> One of the most valuable habits you can develop is to press **Ctrl+S** frequently. Since saving your Vegas project does not affect your ability to undo your edits, there is usually no reason not to save whenever you make significant edits.

In the Save As dialog, use Windows navigation techniques to specify a location on your computer or network drives. Give your file a name in the **File name** box. The first time you save your project, there is only one option available under the **Save as type** drop-down list—*Vegas Project File (*.veg)*—so you don't need to worry about selecting anything. On subsequent visits to the Save As dialog, you have another option—*EDL Text File (*.txt)*—which saves details of all your edits to a text file.

Select the remaining option—the **Copy and trim media with project** check box when you want Vegas to collect all the media you've used to construct your project and save it in the folder you've specified as the location of your project file. This extremely valuable project management tool gathers all of the assets of your project into one location (regardless of the original location of the assets). This prevents you from forgetting where a clip is stored or accidentally deleting a file that you used in a project (which would cause a problem the next time you try to open the project).

Once you've specified the save location and given your project a name, select the **Copy and trim media with project** check box, and then click the **Save** button. The **Copy Media Options** dialog presents you with two choices on how to save the media used in the project. Select the **Copy source media** radio button to save exact copies of all of the media used.

In some cases, you've used only a small portion of a large media file in your project. It might not be necessary for you to save the entire media file with your project, and you can instruct Vegas to trim your media to just the portion you used in the project. You can also save an extra amount at the beginning and end of the section of the media that you actually used. Select the **Create trimmed copies of source media** radio button to save just the portion of the media you used. Enter an amount in the **Extra head and tail (seconds)** box to save more of the file at the beginning and end of the actual area used. This gives you a little more of the media to work with if at some later date you decide you want to edit your project further.

When you've made your choices in the Copy Media Options dialog, click **OK** to complete the save operation.

pt   ### Private Tutor: Cleaning out the Media Pool

Before you save your project with the **Copy and trim media with project** check box selected, make sure that you clean out your project's Media Pool. The Media Pool remembers every media file you added to your project during the editing process—*even if you deleted the file from your project*. If the file still appears in the Media Pool, it will be copied to the save location. This can mean that you end up copying files that you really don't need. To clean the Media Pool of all the files that were not used in the final project, click the **Remove All Unused Media From Project** button, shown in **Figure 8.1** in the Media Pool window or choose **Tools | Clean Media Pool**. If you have some media that you didn't use but still want to keep in your Media Pool for some reason, don't use either of these methods. Instead, right-click the files in the Media Pool you do want to remove, and choose **Remove** from the shortcut menu.

Figure 8.1

Click the **Remove All Unused Media from Project** button to clear your project of media that you deleted from your project.

Remove All Unused
Media from Project

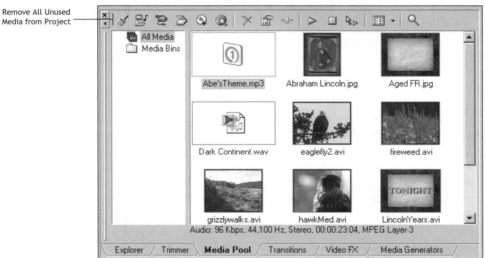

Task 1: Saving your project with trimmed media

In this task, you'll save a Vegas project and copy the media it uses in the process. You'll then add the trimmed media in a project and compare it to the original media to see the results of trimming the copied media.

1. Open *M08Task001.veg* in the *LessonFile\Module08\M08Task001.veg* folder on the companion CD. Play the project and pay particular attention to the audio file.
2. Choose File | Save As.
3. In the Save As dialog, choose the *My Documents* folder on your computer as the **Save in** location. Name the file *VegasTrimTest.veg*.
4. Select the Copy and trim media with project check box.
5. Click **Save**.
6. In the Copy Media Options dialog, select **Create trimmed copies of source media**, and specify "1.0" in the **Extra head and tail (seconds)**.
7. Click **OK**. A progress dialog monitors the saving process.
8. Click the **New** button to start a new project.
9. In the Explorer window, navigate to your *My Documents* folder. Add the file *Dark Continent–000.w64* to the new project. This is the trimmed copy of the media from *M08Task001.veg*. Play the project and note that it includes the audio from *M08Task001.veg* plus the one-second head and tail that you specified in Step 6.
10. Navigate to the companion CD-ROM and add the file *\SampleMedia\Audio\Dark Continent.wav* to a new track. Notice that the original media is much longer than the trimmed copy.

pt Private Tutor: Finding your backup files

As an extra measure of safety, Vegas has two automatic file backup features. First, Vegas saves a backup of your project every five minutes. The backup is saved to the location specified in the **Temporary files folder** box on the **General** tab of the Preferencesdialog. These files have the extension *autosave.veg*, and Vegas deletes them when you properly close the application. Second, every time you save your project, another project file is created along with the main Vegas project. This file, with the extension *veg.bak*, provides you an easy way to go back to your last-saved version of the project. This comes in handy when you want to experiment with edits: if your experiments don't work out, you can always open the *veg.bak* file to go back to the previously saved version.

Lesson 2: Rendering your project

As mentioned, when you save your Vegas project, you create a file that only you are likely to see or hear. When you're ready for others to experience your work, it's time to render your project and possibly print the project to tape or burn it to a CD. This lesson explores the basics of rendering. In the following lesson, you'll learn how to print your videos to videotape.

pt Private Tutor: Understanding rendering

When you render your project, you create a single file based on the instructions you've given Vegas during the editing process. This file can then be played on any computer, as long as the computer has a media player (such as the Windows Media Player) that can read the file. In many cases, you can also bring the file back into a Vegas project. We don't have the space in this book to fully discuss all of the file formats, templates, and customization options available in the Render As dialog. To build your understanding of video-related issues, visit http://www.creativecow.net/articles/spottedeagle_douglas/audio_prep/, or http://www.dv.com/. For audio-related issues, visit http://www.harmony-central.com, or http://www.prorec.com/.

To render your project, choose **File | Render As**. The Render As dialog shown in **Figure 8.2** looks and works much like the Save As dialog. Navigate to the location where you want to save the rendered file. Give the file a name in the **File name** box, and choose the file type you want from the **Save as type** drop-down list. Each file type has a number of predefined templates available from the **Template** drop-down list. If you want to render just a portion of the project, select the **Render loop region only** check box to render just the current loop region in your project. When you've made all of your choices, click **Save**.

Figure 8.2
The Render As dialog lets you choose the location and format of your rendered project.

Private Tutor: Waiting for the render

pt

Rendering video is the most processor-intensive part of working on your project. Complex video projects can take a very long time to render. Remember to build plenty of time into your production schedule to allow for rendering!

Task 2: Rendering your project

This task walks you through the steps required to render your project as a DV file suitable for viewing on another computer. Before you render, you'll establish a loop region so that Vegas renders only that portion of the project.

1. Open *M08Task002.veg* in the *LessonFile\Module08* folder on the companion CD.
2. Double-click the audio event in track 11 to set a loop region.
3. Choose **File | Render As**.
4. Navigate to your *My Documents* folder in the **Save in** drop-down list.
5. Name the file "TheLincolnYears" in the **File name** box.
6. Choose **Video for Windows (*.avi)** from the **Save as type** drop-down list.
7. Choose *NTSC DV* from the **Template** drop-down list.
8. Select the **Render loop region only** check box.
9. Click the **Save** button. When the render is complete, navigate to your *My Documents* folder and double-click the file to watch it in your computer's media player.
10. Keep this project open so you can work on it in the next task.

Vegas allows you to render your project in several formats that are suitable for streaming from your Web site. These formats include:

- **QuickTime (.mov)**—For delivery of video and audio.
- **RealMedia (.rm)**—For delivery of video and audio.
- **Windows Media Audio (.wma)**—For delivery of audio only.
- **Windows Media Video (.wmv)**—For delivery of video files (that could also contain audio).

Private Tutor: Learning more about Web streaming

pt

The subject of streaming audio and video files from your Web pages is another complex issue. For good resources for learning more about streaming technologies, visit http://www.microsoft.com, http://www.real.com, and http://www.apple.com.

Vegas provides several tools to help you prepare your projects for streaming. For instance, you can add metadata to your encoded file to create location markers and synchronize browser commands with the streaming media file. Command markers are embedded into the streaming file and can trigger events while your viewers watch your streaming video. To add a command marker, position the cursor where you want the event to occur, and choose **Insert | Command** (or press **C**).

In the **Command Properties** dialog, choose the type of command you want to insert from the **Command** drop-down list. Type the parameters of the command into the **Parameter** box. Add an optional comment in the **Comment** box. Finally, click **OK** to place the marker. A blue command marker appears at the top of the timeline. Drag the marker to a new position if you decide it is not in the correct place. To edit the marker, right-click the marker tab and choose **Edit** from the shortcut menu.

Two command types are particularly useful. The URL command starts the viewer's browser and displays the page you want them to visit (called a URL flip). To accomplish this, choose **URL** from the **Command** drop-down list and type the Web address of the desired page into the **Parameter** box, as shown in **Figure 8.3**. After you render the file to a streaming format (known as encoding the file) and post it to your Web page, anyone who views or listens to the file is taken to the specified page when the file reaches the location of the command marker.

Figure 8.3
To create a URL flip, choose the URL command type, and then add the Web address to the **Parameter** box.

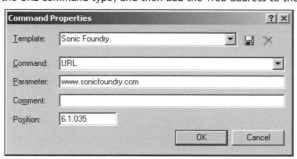

Another useful command type is Text. This command displays captioning with your streaming media file (in WMA or WMV formats only). To do this, position the marker at the beginning of a short phrase of spoken text, choose **TEXT** from the **Command** drop-down list, and type the text into the **Parameter** box. Make another marker for the next phrase of text. Now when visitors view your streaming file (with their Windows Media Player properly configured), they can read along with the spoken text.

Private Tutor: Viewing captioning

The Windows Media Player must be properly configured to view the text you enter in the following task. In Windows Media Player 7, choose **View | Now Playing Tools | Captions**. In Windows Media Player 9, choose **Tools | Options | Security | Run script commands when present**.

Task 3: Using command markers in your streaming media files

In this task, you'll place command markers in your project to create closed captioning and insert a URL flip into your video. You'll then render the project to a format that is suitable for streaming from your Web site.

1. If the file from the last task is no longer open, open *M08Task002.veg* in the *LessonFile\Module08* folder on the companion CD.
2. Click the beginning of the audio event in track 11 to place your cursor there.
3. Press **C**.
4. Choose **Text** from the **Command** drop-down list.
5. Type "A young nation" in the **Parameter** box.
6. Click **OK.**
7. Place additional text command markers at the beginnings of other phrases in the dialog, and type the appropriate text into the **Parameter** boxes.
8. Place a URL command marker just before the point where the video fades out. Type "http://www.historyplace.com/lincoln/" in the **Parameter** box.
9. Render your project as a .wmv file (use the "1 Mbps Video" template).
10. Watch the file in the Windows Media Player. The text commands display the dialog as the movie plays, and if you have an active Internet connection, your browser displays the page specified in Step 8 as the movie fades out.
11. Close this project without saving changes, then view your movie in the Windows Media player.

In a short project, the method you used to add captioning in the previous task works well, but it can get cumbersome in large projects with a lot of dialog. In these cases, first create your text in a tab-delimited, four-column text file (using a text editor or word-processing application). You can also create your text in a spreadsheet application for this purpose. In the four columns, enter the following:

- **Column 1**—Enter "00:00:00:00" for every line of captioning.
- **Column 2**—Enter "TEXT" to specify the command marker type.
- **Column 3**—Enter the text that should appear as the captioning for this line.
- **Column 4**—Enter the line number (for instance, "Line 001" for the first line of dialog).

pt Private Tutor: Using *Vegas Captioning Shell.txt*

The Vegas application CD contains a file named *Vegas Captioning Shell.txt*. This text file is a template that you can use to create your tab-delimited file. Paste or type each phrase of your closed captioning into the space between the "TEXT" and "Line XXX" fields. Delete any extra lines or add more lines if you need them. **Figure 8.4** shows the *Vegas Captioning Shell.txt* document after a few lines of information have been added to it.

Figure 8.4
Add your information to Vegas Captioning Shell.txt, then copy and paste the information into the Edit Details window.

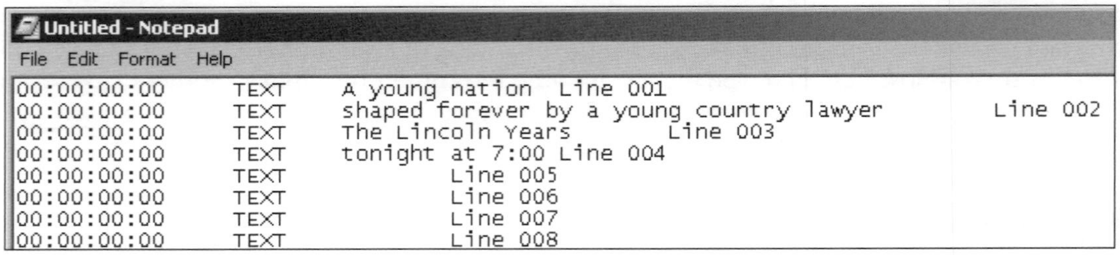

Copy the text to the Windows clipboard. In Vegas, choose **View | Edit Details** (or press **Alt+4**) to open the Edit Details window. Choose **Commands** and **All Fields** from the **Show** drop-down list. Click the blank rectangular box to the left of the box labeled "Position" to select all fields in the window. Press **Ctrl+V** to paste your script into the window. Click the column heading for the Comment column to sort the captions by the Comment line and ensure the proper order. Click the box labeled "1." Finally, play your project, and just before the first line of narration, press **Ctrl+K**. This places the first command marker at that spot. Just before the second line of narration, press **Ctrl+K** again to place the next command marker. Continue until all of the markers have been properly placed. If you didn't get a marker in exactly the right spot, drag the marker tab to the proper position.

Task 4: Using a text script to add multiple command markers

This task shows you how to add a script to the Vegas Edit Details window to help speed up the process of adding command markers.

1. Open *M08Task002.veg* in the *LessonFile\Module08* folder on the companion CD.
2. In a text editor, open the file *\LessonFile\Module08\Vegas Captioning Shell.txt* on the companion CD.
3. In the text file, click near the midpoint of the space between "TEXT" and "Line 001" in the first line of text.
4. Type "A young nation."
5. In the second line of text, type "shaped forever by a young country lawyer." In the third line, type "The Lincoln Years." In the fourth line, type "Tonight at seven." See **Figure 8.4**.
6. Copy theses four text lines onto the Windows clipboard.
7. In Vegas, choose **View | Edit Details** if the Edit Details window is not already open.
8. In the Edit Details window, choose **Commands** and **All Fields** from the **Show** drop-down list.
9. Click the blank rectangular box to the left of the word "Position."
10. Press **Ctrl+V**. Notice in your project that you can see only one blue command marker. Since the markers all have the same position (00:00:00:00), you can see only the one on the top.
11. Click the column heading for the **Comment** column. You may need to scroll to the right in the Edit Details window to see this column. This sorts the captions by the numbers entered in the **Comment** column.
12. Click the box labeled "1" in the Edit Details window to select that row.
13. Play the project. When playback reaches the beginning of the first line of dialog, press **Ctrl+K**. Repeat this command at the beginning of each remaining line of dialog.
14. Zoom in to see that the markers have been properly placed.
15. Render the project as a .wmv file and watch it in the Windows Media Player.

pt Private Tutor: Previewing your project in the appropriate player

You can preview your video as a rendered file without leaving Vegas. This is particularly helpful when you want to see and hear exactly how an edit is going to look and sound as a streaming file. To preview your project in your target player, choose **Tools | Preview in Player**. From the **Preview as** drop-down list, choose the file type you want to preview. Choose the appropriate template and select the **Render loop region only** check box to view just the portion of the project within the loop region. Click **OK**. After the rendering process finishes, Vegas starts the media player associated with the file type you chose in the **Preview as** drop-down list and plays the video.

Lesson 3: Printing to tape

You'll often want to deliver your video projects on videotape. In this lesson, you'll learn how to transfer your video from a file on your computer (either a rendered file or a Vegas project) to DV tape so that you can play it back on your DV camcorder or tape deck.

You can use Sonic Foundry Video Capture to print the rendered file to tape. In order to do this, you must first render the project as an .avi file in DV format. Turn on your recording device (camcorder set to VCR or VTR mode, or DV deck), insert a blank DV tape into it, and connect it to your computer via an IEEE-1394 cable.

Choose **File | Capture Video** to open Sonic Foundry Video Capture as shown in **Figure 8.5**. Click **Cancel** to dismiss the Verify Tape Name dialog. Click the **Print to Tape** tab. Choose **File | Open** and navigate to the DV file you want to print to tape. When you click the **Open** button, the file appears on the right side of the video capture utility. Click the **Record to Device** button. Your camcorder or DV deck begins recording and stops when the entire file has been recorded to the tape.

Figure 8.5

Use the Sonic Foundry Video Capture application to print a rendered file to DV tape.

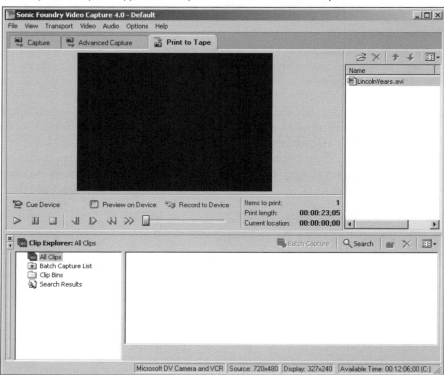

Task 5: Printing a rendered file to tape

In this task, you'll open a rendered file in Sonic Foundry Video Capture and print the file to a DV tape deck or camcorder.

1. Connect your DV camcorder or tape deck to your computer via an IEEE-1394 cable.
2. Choose **File | Capture Video**.
3. In Sonic Foundry Video Capture, click the **Print to Tape** tab.
4. Choose **File | Open**.
5. Navigate to and open the file *TheLincolnYears.avi* you created earlier and saved in your *MyDocuments* folder.
6. Click the **Record to Device** button.

pt Private Tutor: Printing a batch of files to tape

You can open several files at once in Sonic Foundry Video Capture. This allows you to set up a batch of files that you want to print to tape. Video Capture prints the first file in the list to tape, then moves on to the second, third, and so on. This type of batch print-to-tape can be a huge time saver because it can be set up and run without constant supervision.

You can also print your Vegas projects to tape directly from the timeline without opening Video Capture utility. This can save a significant amount of time for projects in which you've used mostly DV media because Vegas renders only those portions of your project that are not already in the DV format. When you're ready to print the project to tape, choose **Tools | Print Video to DV Tape**. If prompted to select a device, click **Yes** to go to the **Video Device** tab of the **Preferences** dialog. From the **Device** drop-down list, choose **OHCI Compliant IEEE 1394/DV** and click **OK**. Follow the steps in the Print to Tape wizard to complete the process.

Task 6: Printing to tape from the Vegas timeline

In this task, you'll print your project to DV tape directly from the Vegas timeline.

1. With your recording device ready, choose **Tools | Print Video to DV Tape**.
2. In the **Conform Timeline to DV Format** page of the Print to Tape wizard, choose the appropriate option from the **DV template** drop-down list. Check the documentation from your camera or DV deck to see if your DV device is an NTSC (the format used in the US) or PAL (the format used in many parts of Europe) device and pick the appropriate DV template.
3. If you want to print the portion of your project included within the loop region, select the **Render loop region only** check box.
4. Click **Next**.
5. The Leader and Trailer page adds a test pattern, tone, and leader and trailer (a black video screen) to your project. Change the settings and click **Next**, or simply click **Next** to accept the defaults.
6. In the **Device Setup** page, accept the default settings to give Vegas control over your recording device. Click **Finish**. Vegas renders the portions of your project that are not already in DV format (if over 80% of your project needs to be rendered, a dialog asks whether you want to continue). When the render is complete, the audio portion of your project is rendered to the Sonic Foundry Wave64 (.w64) format.
7. When both the audio and video portions are rendered, Vegas prints the project to your DV tape.

Conclusion

In this lesson, you've taken the final steps in creating your Vegas projects. You learned how to save your project, render the project to a computer file format that can be played on other computers, and print the project to video tape so anyone can watch it on a television. You also learned a little bit about streaming media and the powerful tools that Vegas provides for creating video and audio that you can stream from your Web site. You learned how to embed metadata to create closed captioning that your viewers can read with the Windows Media Player.

Although Vegas is simple to use, it is a very powerful application. We have only scratched the surface of its capabilities in this book. But you now know enough to get some very serious video and audio production done. Take time to explore those areas that we didn't dive into here, and dig deeper into those subjects on which we touched only lightly. Use the Vegas help files and the PDF manual often for even more ideas—we did! Most of all, let your imagination run wild, and have fun creating rich multimedia with Vegas.

Exercises

1. True or false: After the first time you save your Vegas project, you must choose **File | Save As** to access the Save As dialog.

2. True or false: Once you save your project, anyone can view your video project on their computer as long as they have the proper media player.

3. Which of the following describes what happens when you copy trimmed media during the save process?

    a. Vegas clears your Vegas project of all media that you imported into Vegas but ended up not using in the final project.

    b. Vegas trims your project down to a user-defined length.

    c. Vegas places trimmed copies of the media files you used in your project in the location where you saved the project file.

    d. Vegas lowers the volume of all the audio in your project to prevent clipping.

4. True or false: Every time you save your project, Vegas creates a backup file so you can always go back to your previously saved version of the project.

5. Which of the following allows you to render your project?

    a. Click the **Render Project** button.

    b. Choose **File | Render As.**

    c. Press **Ctrl+R**.

    d. Choose **Options | Render As**.

6. Which type of command marker do you use in a streaming media file to automatically take your viewer's browser to a different Web page?

    a. URL

    b. TEXT

    c. HotSpotBrowse

    d. HotSpotSeek

7. True or false: When rendering a file, the .rm or .wmv formats are good choices if you want to allow visitors to your Web site to view your video.

8. True or false: To print your project to tape, you must first render the project as a DV file.

9. Which of the following is one advantage of using Sonic Foundry Video Capture to print your project to tape?

    a. You don't have to render the project before printing it to tape.

    b. You can click the **Print loop region only** button to print just a portion of your project to tape.

    c. Vegas can print the project to tape at twice normal speed.

    d. You can set up a batch and print several files in one operation.

10. True or false: You should render your project in a streaming file format in order to dramatically reduce the time it takes to print to tape from the Sonic Foundry Video Capture.

11. Which of the following is not an advantage of printing to tape from the timeline?

    a. You can set Vegas up to print a batch of files.

    b. You don't have to wait through a separate render process before printing to tape.

    c. It can be significantly faster if most of the clips in your project are already in DV format.

    d. You may be able to save storage space on your computer because you may not need to render the entire project before you print it.

12. Draw a line connecting the keyboard shortcut to the action it performs

a. Ctrl+S	Drop a command marker.
b. C	Open the Edit Details window.
c. Ctrl+K	Save (if you previously saved your project).
d. Alt+4	Save As (if you've never saved your project before).
e. Ctrl+S	Drop the next command marker at the current cursor position.

Essays

1. Describe both methods of printing to tape and include discussion of when one method might be more appropriate than the other.

2. Describe why it is important to check your Media Pool before saving your project with the Copy Trimmed Media option. Describe how what you find in your Media Pool affects what you do next.

Index

W

Waveform, 21, 25, 41, 86
Web streaming, 154
Window docking area
    Creating floating windows over, 10
    Defined, 9
    Hiding, 8, 11
    Resizing, 8
    Tabs, 9
Windows
    Audio Plug-In, 119
    Edit Details, 156, 157
    Explorer, 14
    Explorer, 9, 14
    Media Pool, 41, 130, 151
    Mixer, 9, 18, 117
    Plug-Ins, 50

    Resizing, 11, 50
    Transitions, 10, 137
    Video Event FX, 51
    Video Preview, 9, 20
Windows Classic Wave Driver, 42
Windows Record Control, 40

Z

Zoom
    Horizontal scroll, 81
    in/out time, 79
    In/Out Time, 80
    in/out track height, 79
    Mouse wheel, 80
    Track height, 81
    Zoom Edit tool, 79
    Zoom time controls, 80